ISBN 978-0-428-08242-0
PIBN 11243331

This book is a reproduction of an important historical work. Forgotten Books uses state-of-the-art technology to digitally reconstruct the work, preserving the original format whilst repairing imperfections present in the aged copy. In rare cases, an imperfection in the original, such as a blemish or missing page, may be replicated in our edition. We do, however, repair the vast majority of imperfections successfully; any imperfections that remain are intentionally left to preserve the state of such historical works.

English
Français
Deutsche
Italiano
Español
Português

www.forgottenbooks.com

Mythology Photography **Fiction**
Fishing Christianity **Art** Cooking
Essays Buddhism Freemasonry
Medicine **Biology** Music **Ancient**
Egypt Evolution Carpentry Physics
Dance Geology **Mathematics** Fitness
Shakespeare **Folklore** Yoga Marketing
Confidence Immortality Biographies
Poetry **Psychology** Witchcraft
Electronics Chemistry History **Law**
Accounting **Philosophy** Anthropology
Alchemy Drama Quantum Mechanics
Atheism Sexual Health **Ancient History**
Entrepreneurship Languages Sport
Paleontology Needlework Islam
Metaphysics Investment Archaeology
Parenting Statistics Criminology
Motivational

Historic, Archive Document

Do not assume content reflects current scientific knowledge, policies, or practices.

sta

United States
Department of
Agriculture

Economic
Research
Service

LPS-12
August 1984

Livestock and Poultry

Outlook and Situation Report

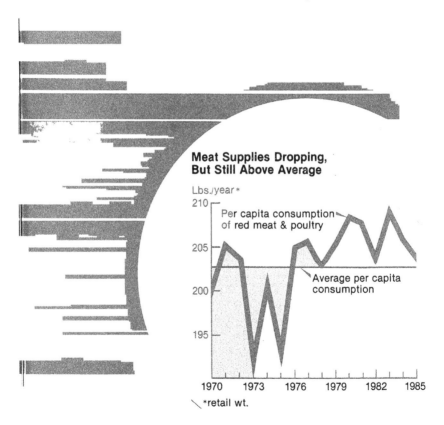

**Meat Supplies Dropping,
But Still Above Average**

Lbs./year *

Per capita consumption
of red meat & poultry

Average per capita
consumption

1970   1973   1976   1979   1982   1985

*retail wt.

Contents

Situation Coordinator
Ronald Gustafson (202) 447-8636

Principal Contributors
John Nalivka (Cattle)
Leland Southard (Hogs and Sheep)
Allen Baker (Poultry)
Karen Parham (Retail Prices and Consumption)

Statistical Assistants
Evelyn Blazer (Livestock)
Eunice Armstrong (Poultry)

Electronic Word Processing
Trayci D. Massey

National Economics Division
Economic Research Service
U.S. Department of Agriculture
Washington, D.C. 20250

Approved by the World Agricultural Outlook Board. Summary released August 1, 1984. The next summary of the **Livestock and Poultry Outlook and Situation** is scheduled for release on September 28, 1984. Summaries of Outlook and Situation reports may be accessed electronically. For details call (402) 472-1892 or (301) 588-1572. Full reports, including tables, are provided by the system on (402) 472-1892.

The present forecasts will be updated in the World Agricultural Supply and Demand Estimates scheduled for release on August 13 and September 13, 1984.

The **Livestock and Poultry Outlook and Situation** is published 6 times a year. Annual subscription: $15.00 U.S., $18.75 foreign. Order from the Superintendent of Documents, U.S. Government Printing Office, Washington, D.C. 20402. Make checks payable to the Superintendent of Documents.

Current subscribers will receive renewal notices from the Government Printing Office approximately 90 days before their subscriptions expire. Notices will be sent ONLY ONCE and should be returned promptly to ensure uninterrupted service.

Summary

Cattle numbers on July 1 were 1 percent lower than a year earlier, showing a continued modest decline. Poor returns, extended drought in some areas, and financial problems have all contributed to the herd reduction. The beef cow inventory was down 1 percent from 1983 and 2 percent from 1982. In spite of prospects for reduced meat supplies and higher prices through mid-1985, producers have again cut the number of heifers they are retaining for breeding. The 1984 calf crop is expected to fall 2 percent from a year ago, making this the fourth consecutive year of decline. The supply of feeder cattle remains ample to meet the increased feedlot demand.expected this fall as the larger grain crop is harvested.

Poor returns to turkey producers during the early hatching season could spell lower turkey output in the second half than previously anticipated. Consequently, wholesale turkey prices may average above a year earlier for the remainder of 1984.

Total red meat and poultry production for the rest of the year will remain near first-half levels. For all of 1984, red meat production is likely to be about 2 percent less than in 1983, while poultry production may be about 2 percent more. Next year, red meat output may decline about 3 percent. However, poultry production may expand around 5 percent. Total meat production will likely fall slightly in 1985. However, red meat and poultry consumption in 1984 and 1985 will likely remain above the 1970-83 average of 203 pounds per capita.

Red meat prices will rise moderately as supplies, especially pork, decline through at least mid-1985. Prices for Choice beef may move up 3 to 5 percent next year, compared with about 3 percent this year. Retail pork prices will be about unchanged this year, but they could climb 10 to 14 percent in 1985. As supplies of broilers and turkeys increase through next year, wholesale prices for both may fall from their higher 1984 averages.

Egg production this spring was almost the same as in spring 1983. But, output is likely to remain above a year earlier through 1985 as more pullets enter the laying flock. Through the middle of next year, wholesale egg prices will probably stay well below the averages of the last 12 months.

Item	1983		1984					1985	
	IV	Annual	I	II[1]	III[2]	IV[2]	Annual[2]	I	Annual
					Million lbs				
PRODUCTION									
Beef	5,962	23,060	5,709	5,819	5,875	5,575	22,978	5,500	22,375
% change	+2	+3	+3	+5	−2	−6	0	−4	−3
Pork	4,206	15,117	3,737	3,670	3,300	3,725	14,432	3,450	14,100
% change	+16	+7	+7	−3	−10	−11	−5	−8	−2
Lamb & mutton	91	367	98	92	85	80	355	85	320
% change	−2	+3	+5	+3	10	−12	−3	−13	−10
Veal	117	428	116	113	100	105	434	100	385
% change	+6	+1	+13	+15	−9	−10	+1	−14	−11
Total red meat	10,376	38,972	9,660	9,694	9,360	9,485	38,199	9,135	37,180
% change	+7	+5	+5	+2	−5	−9	−2	−5	−3
Broilers[3]	2,917	12,389	3,075	3,330	3,300	3,080	12,785	3,250	13,350
% change	0	+3	+1	+2	+5	+6	+3	+6	+4
Turkeys[3]	759	2,563	431	585	750	745	2,511	460	2,630
% change	0	+4	−7	+1	−1	−2	−2	+7	+5
Total poultry[4]	3,781	15,453	3,619	4,050	4,175	3,935	15,779	3,850	16,520
% change	−1	+3	−1	+2	+4	+4	+2	+6	+5
Total red meat & poultry	14,157	54,425	13,279	13,744	13,535	13,420	53,978	12,985	53,700
% change	+5	+4	+3	+2	−3	−5	−1	−2	−1
					Million dozen				
Eggs	1,418	5,655	1,401	1,408	1,430	1,460	5,699	1,450	5,820
% change	−4	−2	−2	−0	+2	+3	+1	+3	+2
					Dollars per cwt				
PRICES									
Choice steers, Omaha, 900-1100 lb	60.61	62.37	67.58	66.01	64-67	65-69	65-68	68-72	67-73
Barrows & gilts, 7 mkts	42.18	47.71	47.68	48.91	53-56	52-56	50-52	56-60	55-61
Slaugh. lambs, Ch., San Ang.	57.63	57.63	59.29	63.09	60-63	61-65	60-63	62-66	61-67
					Cents per lb				
Broilers, 9-city avg.[5]	55.2	[8]	61.8	56.4	52-55	50-54	55-57	53-57	51-57
Turkeys, NY[6]	69.4	60.5	67.7	66.9	71-74	72-76	69-72	68-72	64-70
					Cents per doz				
Eggs New York[7]	91.3	75.2	103.4	83.4	70-74	68-72	82-84	66-70	66-72

[1]Preliminary. [2]Forecast. [3]Federally inspected. [4]Includes broilers, turkeys, and mature chickens. [5]Wholesale weighted average. [6]Wholesale, 8- to 16-pound young hens. [7]Cartoned, consumer Grade A large, sales to volume buyers. [8]The 9-city price has been discontinued; starting with second-quarter 1983, the broiler price is the new 12-city average. Quarterly data not comparable to compute average.

FACTORS AFFECTING LIVESTOCK AND POULTRY

Economy Likely Strong Through Mid-1985

Relatively strong economic growth is likely to support meat prices through the remainder of 1984. While growth rates of first-half 1984 are expected to gradually slow through 1985, the economy seems likely to remain strong until at least mid-1985. Low inflation rates and continued increases in employment should result in rising real incomes and continued consumer confidence. Greater consumer purchasing power through mid-1985 will coincide with total red meat and poultry production which will be below the record levels of a year earlier. But, supplies will be big enough to temper meat price increases. Larger meat supplies are likely in second-half 1985 when growth in the economy could be cooling.

Feed Costs To Decline

Sharp increases in planted acreages and improved growing conditions in the United States are likely to result in substantial stock rebuilding, particularly for feed grains. Global coarse grain supplies in 1984/85 are expected to be the second highest on record. U.S. exports are likely to be limited by large world supplies and the strong dollar.

Domestic livestock feeding is expected to expand from the depressed levels in 1983/84, as higher livestock and poultry prices and lower feed costs improve feeding margins. Wheat supplies will remain large, but feed use is likely to decline from the near-record volumes recorded since last spring. Prices for wheat averaged $3.54 a bushel in 1983/84 and are expected to range from $3.25 to $3.50 in 1984/1985. However, corn prices should fall much more than wheat, returning the wheat-corn price ratios to a more normal relationship. The farm price of corn is expected to average $3.25 a bushel for 1983/84, but it may average between the $2.55 loan rate and $3.05 next year.

Regional feeding activity will also influence feed use and prices of corn versus wheat. Sharply reduced grain supplies in the North Central region have significantly cut livestock feeding activity there. Moreover, declining land values, financial weakness, and relatively high cash grain prices may slow livestock feeding activity, even when grain supplies improve.

Reduced feeding activity may also be presaged by indications that both corn and sorghum silage acreage are likely to decline this fall. Producers indicated in June that they intended to plant 79.94 million acres of corn. Given this acreage, past relationships indicate that 7.3 million corn acres would be harvested for silage, making 1984 the fourth consecutive year of decline. A similar examination of the sorghum acreage indicates that 981,000 acres will likely be harvested for silage, down nearly 400,000 from a year ago, again making this the fourth consecutive year of decline.

These figures reinforce indications that crop-livestock producers are unwilling to accept the higher risk of marketing their grain through livestock, rather than the cash market.

Forage Conditions Mixed

Pasture and range feed conditions on July 1 were good to excellent, which is near the average but below the very favorable conditions of a year ago. However, conditions in Texas were rated in severe drought. Moisture and cooler weather improved conditions in many other areas during July, especially in the Southeast. However, central Texas and much of Montana remained severely dry in late July. In much of the remainder of the country, particularly the Mountain, Northern Plains, and North Central States, forage conditions were very favorable on July 1.

LIVESTOCK AND RED MEATS

Cattle

Cattle producers have continued to reduce their herds, as indicated by a 1-percent decline in the July 1 cattle and calves inventory. Compelled by tight forage supplies in some areas and financial difficulties in the cow-calf sector of the beef industry, producers sent over 4 million cows to slaughter during the first half of the year, a 20-percent increase over first-half last year. The increased cow slaughter was offset somewhat, though, by a larger percentage of heifers entering the herd during January-June.

Cows and Heifers That Have Calved Down 1 Percent

The July 1 inventory of all cattle and calves was estimated at 122 million head. The number of cows and heifers that had calved was estimated at 48.95 million, down 1 percent from last year. The number of heifers entering the herd during January-June was 4.7 million—43.9 percent of the replacement heifers on hand on January 1. This compares to 39.8 percent for the same period last year and 32.2 percent in 1982.

Table 2.—July 1 cattle inventory

Class	1982	1983	1984	1984/83
	1,000 head			% change
Cattle and calves	124,140	123,540	121,950	−1.3
Cows and heifers that have calved	49,990	49,600	48,950	−1.3
Beef cows	38,970	38,480	38,100	−1.0
Milk cows	11,020	11,120	10,850	−2.4
Heifers 500 lb and over	18,550	18,570	18,600	+.2
For beef cow replacement	6,120	5,800	5,600	−3.4
For milk cow replacement	4,780	4,880	4,950	+1.4
Other heifer	7,650	7,890	8,050	+2.0
Steers 500 lb and over	16,340	16,840	16,400	−2.6
Bulls 500 lb and over	2,610	2,560	2,500	−2.3
Heifers, steers, and bulls under 500 lb	36,650	35,970	35,000	−1.3
Calf crop[1]	44,420	44,093	43,400	−1.6

[1]For the current year, the calf crop is the number of calves born before July 1 plus the number expected to be born on and after July 1.

3

Table 3.—Heifers entering cow herd January-June and July-December

Year	January 1 cow inventory	Intended herd replacements January 1	Total[1] disappearance Jan.-June	July 1 cow inventory	Heifers entering herd Jan.-June	Percent entering herd	Intended herd replacements July 1	Total[2] disappearance July-Dec.	January 1 cow inventory following yr.	Heifers entering herd July-Dec.	Percent entering herd
			1,000 head			*Percent*			*1,000 head*		*Percent*
1973	52,553	11,306	3,550	54,037	5,034	44.5	11,144	3,496	54,478	3,937	35.3
1974	54,478	12,134	3,625	56,960	6,107	50.3	11,780	4,702	56,931	4,673	39.7
1975	56,931	12,971	5,212	58,053	6,336	48.8	11,306	7,197	54,974	4,118	36.4
1976	54,971	11,148	5,628	53,938	4,595	41.2	10,475	5,811	52,441	4,314	41.2
1977	52,441	10,414	5,221	52,190	4,970	47.7	9,846	5,429	49,635	2,874	29.2
1978	49,635	9,744	4,961	48,413	3,739	38.4	9,340	4,253	47,852	3,692	39.5
1979	47,852	9,459	3,413	47,815	3,376	35.7	9,885	3,235	47,865	3,285	33.2
1980	47,865	10,097	3,304	49,941	5,380	53.3	10,214	3,748	49,586	3,393	33.2
1981	49,586	10,481	3,599	51,004	5,017	47.9	10,861	3,788	50,331	3,115	28.7
1982	50,331	11,147	3,926	49,990	3,585	32.2	10,900	4,183	49,154	3,347	30.7
1983	49,154	10,876	3,887	49,600	4,333	39.8	10,680	4,457	48,800	3,657	34.2
1984	48,800	10,736	4,565	48,950	4,715	43.9	10,550				

[1]Death loss calculated as 1 percent of January 1 cow inventory plus estimated commercial cow slaughter. [2]Death loss calculated as 1/2 percent of January 1 cow inventory plus estimated commercial cow slaughter.

The number of "other heifers" (not held for replacements) reported was 8 million head, up 2 percent from last year. Some of these may have been reported on January 1 as replacement heifers. However, because of poor returns so far this year, they will not enter the breeding herd and were reported as other heifers in the recent inventory. They will likely be placed on feed this summer and early fall or be slaughtered as nonfeds.

The estimated 1984 calf crop is down 2 percent to 43.4 million head, from 44.1 million in 1983. This calf crop is 88.9 percent of the January 1 cow herd, compared to the 89.7 calf crop ratio in 1983. Two factors may have influenced the decline. First, conception rates may have been lowered last summer during the breeding season by the extreme heat and drought. Second, the drought resulted in reduced forage supplies last summer and fall, while cold weather this winter raised supplemental feeding requirements.

Table 4.—U.S. federally inspected cow slaughter by region, January-June

Standard federal regions[1]	1983	1984	Change	Percent change
	1,000 head			*Percent*
1 & 2[2]	162.0	158.0	-4.0	-2.5
3	212.1	270.0	+58.4	+27.5
4	424.2	477.0	+52.8	+12.4
5	666.9	821.7	+154.8	+23.2
6	535.5	685.6	+150.1	+28.0
7	565.2	751.2	+186.0	+32.9
8	216.0	229.8	+13.8	+6.4
9	265.7	304.0	+38.3	+14.4
10	178.5	201.3	+22.8	+12.8
U.S.[3]	3,226.1	3,899.0	+672.9	+20.9

[1]States included in regions are as follows: 1-ME, NH, VT, MA, CT & RI; 2-NY & NJ; 3-PA, WV, VA & DE-MD; 4-KY, TN, NC, SC, GA, AL, MS & FL; 5-MI, OH, IN, IL, WI & MN; 6-TX, OK, NM, AR & LA; 7-IA, NB, KS & MO; 8-MT, WY, CO, UT, ND & SD; 9-CA, NV, AZ & HA; 10-ID, OR, WA. [2]Region 1 combined with region 2 to avoid disclosing individual operations. [3]Totals may not add due to rounding.

Table 5.—Commercial cattle slaughter[1] and production

Year	Steers and heifers			Cows	Bulls and stags	Total	Average dressed weight	Commercial production[2]
	Fed	Nonfed	Total					
	1,000 head						*Lb*	*Mil. lb*
1982:								
I	6,148	620	6,768	1,738	173	8,679	629	5,455
II	5,997	746	6,743	1,685	214	8,642	621	5,363
III	6,660	542	7,202	1,787	225	9,214	622	5,730
IV	6,097	861	6,958	2,144	206	9,308	625	5,818
Year	24,902	2,769	27,671	7,354	818	35,843	624	22,366
1983:								
I	6,419	424	6,846	1,701	188	8,732	633	5,527
II	6,367	581	6,948	1,694	209	8,851	628	5,556
III	6,799	621	7,420	1,908	220	9,548	630	6,015
IV	6,145	888	7,033	2,294	191	9,518	626	5,962
Year	25,730	2,514	28,244	7,597	808	36,649	629	23,060
1984:[3]								
I	6,467	456	6,923	2,080	165	9,168	623	5,708
II	6,488	647	7,135	1,998	208	9,341	623	5,819

[1]Classes estimated. [2]May not add due to rounding. [3]Preliminary.

Dairy Cow Slaughter Declines
From First Quarter

Dairy cow slaughter remained above beef cow slaughter through the first week of March, accounting for 50-56 percent of federally inspected (FI) cow slaughter each week since January 1. Then, beginning in the second week of March, beef cow slaughter began to outpace dairy cow slaughter, and it retained this position for the

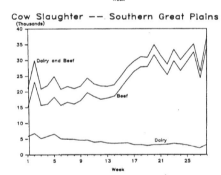

Cow Slaughter — — All Regions
(Thousands)

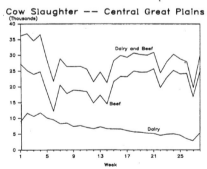

Cow Slaughter — — Southern Great Plains
(Thousands)

Cow Slaughter — — Central Great Plains
(Thousands)

rest of the first half. Total cow slaughter under Federal inspection for the first half was 4 million head—2.23 million beef cows and 1.77 million dairy cows. Most diversion program slaughter has taken place during the first half. The July 1 inventory showed a 2-percent decline in dairy cows. However, milk cow replacement heifers increased 1 percent from a year earlier, to 5 million head.

Second-Half Beef Cow Slaughter
Likely To Decline

For the second consecutive year, beef cow slaughter was high during January-June in the southern Great Plains. Because of tight forage supplies resulting from a continued drought this year, producers sent 29 percent more cows to slaughter than a year earlier. In 1983, cow slaughter was up 19 percent from the year before, also because of the drought.

Cow slaughter in the Northern Plains was also large during first-half 1984, with the greater part being beef cows. Total FI cow slaughter was 744,700 head, including 186,500 dairy cows. This region is primarily comprised of mixed crop-livestock operations.

Because cow slaughter has remained heavy throughout the second quarter, it may not increase this fall as much as usual. Three factors support a forecast of declining cow slaughter:

● the herd will be well culled going into the fourth quarter;

● additional hay acreage is expected to be harvested, and forage conditions will probably be mostly good the rest of the year; and

● producers may begin to rebuild or at least stabilize the beef cow herd with the expectation of higher prices in 1985.

The average dressed weight of cows slaughtered in June was 490 pounds, 20 below last year and the lowest for June since 1978. This lower dressed weight indicates cows in poor condition, reflecting the severity of the drought in the Southwest and the late grazing season in many other areas because of the cool wet spring.

Cattle Herd Expansion
Not Likely Until 1986

After being in a holding pattern for the past 3 years, the cattle cycle is not likely to enter the expansion phase before 1986. Although a large percentage of heifers have calved and entered the herd over the past year, an even larger number of cows have been culled from the herd. The percentage of heifers retained might have been larger and might have indicated herd expansion if producers had not been constrained by financial problems or by lack of forage. In addition, the reported number of other heifers was large, suggesting that producers may have initially intended to hold a larger number of replacements to build their herds.

Given the likelihood that good forage conditions will continue in most regions and cattle prices will be higher this fall, the cattle industry may begin an expansion. A larger number of replacements may be held this fall, to

5

Table 6.—Federally inspected cattle slaughter

Week ended	Cattle		Steers		Cows			
					Total		Dairy	Dairy as percent of total
	1983	1984	1983	1984	1983	1984	1984	
				Thousands				*Percent*
Jan. 1[1]	555	589	268	292	115	133	—	—
8	682	606	299	277	159	164	84	51
15	725	699	337	325	156	180	90	50
22	693	707	329	339	140	163	87	53
29	667	693	325	333	132	169	90	53
Feb. 5	637	657	312	318	119	159	89	56
12	668	689	330	344	126	150	81	54
19	631	683	310	425	126	153	79	51
26	624	666	326	318	114	146	77	52
Mar. 5	621	684	306	329	112	139	72	52
12	615	675	312	324	108	145	69	48
19	628	689	322	342	114	143	68	48
26	608	644	299	319	113	134	67	50
Apr. 2	589	650	283	312	112	139	67	48
9	588	631	287	301	119	135	65	48
16	644	662	333	328	121	143	62	43
23	636	651	316	322	127	148	60	41
30	623	655	326	322	118	147	57	39
May 7	649	666	332	332	127	149	56	37
14	675	712	339	361	126	145	55	38
21	669	730	333	368	127	152	53	35
28	684	743	333	364	130	155	55	35
June 4	591	642	293	317	109	132	46	35
11	690	720	338	361	128	149	51	34
18	675	722	324	363	126	150	52	35
25	658	706	313	336	132	155	53	35
July 2	662	708	325	333	129	157	52	33
9	590	605	304	285	97	112	38	34
16	682	742	330	337	135	168	58	35
23	652		312		127			
30	661		323		126			
Aug. 6	688		329		131			
13	710		338		140			
20	706		338		143			
27	708		339		142			
Sept. 3	735		354		155			
10	644		304		125			
17	759		351		154			
24	721		313		159			
Oct. 1	746		332		167			
8	736		327		165			
15	734		332		165			
22	725		315		172			
29	728		320		180			
Nov. 5	704		302		182			
12	698		318		162			
19	709		309		180			
26	580		268		137			
Dec. 3	702		320		176			
10	732		318		199			
17	704		331		171			
24	625		303		144			

[1] Corresponding date—1983: January 1, 1983; 1984: December 31, 1983.

mid-1985 and to calve in the fall and
6. These additional heifers would begin
e January 1, 1986, inventory. Even
would calve and show up in the inventory
87.

s in Second Quarter
ent

er corn prices hovered around $3.35 per
attle prices dropped, cattle feeding
antly in the Corn Belt. Iowa reported
n feed on July 1, down 32 percent from
ced on feed in the State during the
were down 38 percent from last year.

nd, cattle feeding in the High Plains and
nued at a strong pace during the first
rices declined further relative to corn
eeding has remained strong in wheat
he number of cattle on feed on July 1 in
on head, was up 23 percent from last
was the largest number for the date
cements in the State during the second
percent and marketings of fed cattle rose
a year earlier.

erly reporting States, cattle on feed on
d 8.7 million head, down 4 percent from
e placed on feed during the second quar-
percent (net placements were down 8
etings of fed cattle increased 2 percent
lier.

steers in the heaviest weight category
ent from a year earlier and these cattle
eady been marketed. The two heaviest
ther were up 8 percent, while steers in the

500-699 pound and 700-899 pound categories were down
17 and 9 percent, respectively. Steer calves under 500
pounds on feed on July 1 were up 30 percent from last
year. Heifers and heifer calves on feed were down 10
percent from 1983. Heifer calves under 500 pounds were
down 1 percent, while heifers on feed weighing over 700
pounds were down 11 percent from a year earlier.

Given the distribution of cattle on feed in the various
weight groups, third-quarter production of fed beef will
be about the same as a year earlier. However, fed
slaughter will be offset to some extent by declining
nonfed slaughter through the third quarter.

Fed beef production will likely decline during the fourth
quarter because fewer cattle were placed on feed during
the spring and early summer. However, nonfed slaughter,
although well below a year earlier, will increase seasonally. Some of the heifers not intended for replacements
on the July 1 inventory may be slaughtered as nonfeds
this fall.

Feeder Cattle Supplies
Down 1 Percent

Supplies of feeder cattle on April 1 were down 3 percent,
suggesting that supplies might be tight going into the
fall. However, the July 1 inventory of feeder cattle outside feedlots was down only 1 percent from a year ago.
Yearling cattle outside feedlots on July 1 were up 1.5
percent from a year earlier, while calves outside feedlots
were down 1.5 percent. As placements on feed increase
this fall, feeder cattle supplies should be ample.

Fourth-quarter feeder cattle prices should still average
in the upper $60's range, given the scenario of lower
grain prices and increased cattle feeding this fall. As

Table 7.—7-States cattle on feed, placements, and marketings

On feed	Change previous year	Net placements	Change previous year	Marketings	Change previous year
1,000 head	Percent	1,000 head	Percent	1,000 head	Percent
8,316	+15.5	1,364	−0.9	1,628	+7.0
8,052	+14.1	1,043	−15.0	1,491	+5.5
7,604	+10.7	1,267	−25.6	1,603	+3.6
7,268	+3.5	1,423	−2.3	1,470	+4.0
7,221	+2.2	1,688	−1.3	1,578	+11.7
7,331	−0.4	1,517	+14.2	1,570	+4.0
7,278	+1.4	1,080	−5.0	1,497	+1.0
6,861	+0.4	1,494	−10.5	1,651	−2.2
6,704	−1.7	1,932	+1.1	1,682	+6.8
6,951	−2.8	2,358	−6.3	1,626	+6.5
7,683	−5.6	1,590	−4.6	1,459	−1.8
7,814	−6.1	1,617	+13.7	1,425	−0.3
8,006	−3.7	1,480	+8.5	1,569	−3.6
7,917	−1.7	1,219	+16.9	1,621	+8.7
7,515	−1.2	1,647	+30.0	1,594	−0.6
7,568	+4.1	1,331	−6.5	1,523	+3.6
7,376	+2.1	1,579	−6.5	1,637	+3.7
7,318	−0.2	1,361	−10.3	1,554	−1.0
7,125	−2.1				

7

Table 8.—Cattle on feed, placements, and marketings, 13 States

Item	1982	1983	1984	1984/1983
		1,000 head		% change
On feed April 1	8,818	9,153	9,340	+2
Placements,				
Apr.-June	5,781	5,894	5,572	−5
Marketings,				
Apr.-June	5,209	5,527	5,630	+2
Other disappearance,				
Apr.-June	409	450	582	+29
On feed July 1	8,981	9,070	8,700	−4
Steer & steer				
calves	5,643	5,661	5,640	0
-500 lb	162	171	222	+30
500-699 lb	667	643	533	−17
700-899 lb	2,283	2,083	1,900	−9
900-1,099 lb	2,185	2,299	2,410	+5
1,100 + lb	346	465	575	+24
Heifers & heifer				
calves	3,306	3,380	3,028	−10
-500 lb	117	73	72	−1
500-699 lb	811	667	600	−10
700-899 lb	1,711	1,695	1,497	−12
900 + lb	667	945	859	−9
Cows	32	29	32	+10
Marketings,				
July-Sept.	5,773	5,891	[1]5,995	+2

[1]Intentions.

these conditions carry over to next spring, yearling steer prices will likely be in the low $70's. Cattle feeding activity will probably remain strong in the Southwest into next year. However, even with lower-priced corn, producers in the Corn Belt may be less willing to accept the additional risk of cattle feeding. In addition, financial problems in the region may have made agricultural lenders cautious. For those operators with sizeable outstanding loans, lenders may prefer that they sell corn rather than borrow money to purchase feeder cattle.

Production Lower, Prices Stronger

Second-half commercial beef production is expected to decline only about 1 percent from first-half 1984. But it will be down about 4 percent from the large second-half 1983 production. Further declines will likely occur during the first 6 months of next year, which could be 5 to 7 percent under first-half 1984. Production for all of 1985 may be down 2 to 4 percent from this year.

With pork production expected to decline through 1984 and into 1985, Choice steer prices will likely strengthen next year. Prices for Choice fed steers at Omaha will probably average near $66 per cwt through mid-fall. Prices in 1985 may average in the high $60's to low $70's. Most of the price strength will likely come next spring. Omaha Choice steers could be bid into the low $70's. Fed cattle prices at Omaha are normally somewhat lower than at Amarillo. However, given the large number of cattle on feed in the High Plains and the reduced feeding activity in the Corn Belt, prices at Amarillo may be lower than in Omaha.

Prices for yearling feeder steers at Kansas City have averaged about a $1 discount to fed steers at Omaha during the first half of 1984, due to high grain prices and poor feeding returns in the Corn Belt. The discount was even greater in the Amarillo area. Stocker demand for cattle was weaker in the High Plains because of the drought in Texas. Yearling steers will likely begin to sell at a premium to Choice fed steers in late summer as grain prices decline. This premium is expected to be maintained into 1985.

Utility cow prices will maintain their spring-early summer strength through the second half of this year and into 1985, picking up even a little more next year. Prices for Utility cows at Omaha averaged over $42 per cwt this spring, and only modest declines are likely in the second half. Cow culling will likely decline greatly next year if a herd expansion begins this fall, thus supporting higher Utility cow prices.

Table 9.—13-States cattle on feed, placements, marketings, and other disappearance

Year	Cattle on feed[1]	Change previous year	Placed on feed	Change previous year	Fed cattle marketed	Change previous year	Other disappear-ance	Change previous year
	1,000 head	Percent	1,000 head	Percent	1,000 head	Percent	1,000 head	Percent
1982:								
I	9,028	−8.3	5,572	15.7	5,443	−2.1	339	−22.6
II	8,818	1.8	5,781	3.4	5,209	1.9	409	−17.7
III	8,981	3.9	5,846	10.8	5,773	5.9	254	−1.2
IV	8,800	7.2	7,216	15.5	5,374	5.6	371	8.8
Year	—	—	24,415	11.3	21,799	2.7	1,373	−10.1
1983:								
I	10,271	13.8	5,027	−9.8	5,694	4.6	451	33.0
II[2]	9,153	3.8	5,894	2.0	5,527	6.1	450	10.0
III	9,067	1.0	5,586	−4.4	5,890	2.0	298	17.3
IV	8,465		7,252	+.4	5,416	.8	393	5.9
Year	—	—	23,771	−2.6	22,545	3.4	1,592	16.0
1984:								
I	9,908	−3.5	5,511	+9.6	5,714	+0.4	365	−19.1
II	9,340	+2.0	5,572	−5.5	5,630	+1.9	582	+29.3

[1]Beginning of quarter. [2]Revised.

Table 10.—Great Plains custom cattle feeding: Selected costs at current rates[1]

Purchased during Marketed during	Sept. 83 Mar. 84	Oct. Apr.	Nov. May	Dec. June	Jan. 84 July	Feb. Aug.	Mar. Sept.	Apr. Oct.	May Nov.	June Dec.
					Dollars per head					
Expenses:										
600-lb feeder steer	346.32	345.24	372.00	396.72	403.92	409.86	407.82	390.48	365.64	361.68
Transportation to feedlot (300 miles)	3.96	3.96	3.96	3.96	3.96	3.96	3.96	3.96	3.96	3.96
Commission	3.00	3.00	3.00	3.00	3.00	3.00	3.00	3.00	3.00	3.00
Feed:										
Milo (1,500 lb)	86.40	83.40	82.50	81.75	80.10	77.70	80.40	84.90	85.65	86.85
Corn (1,500 lb)	93.75	94.20	93.75	93.75	93.30	92.70	95.10	99.30	99.75	99.30
Cottonseed meal (400 lb)	58.00	62.00	62.00	64.00	68.00	64.00	64.00	64.00	62.00	60.00
Alfalfa hay (800 lb)	52.40	50.80	54.40	54.40	56.80	60.40	53.60	57.60	54.40	55.20
Total feed cost	290.55	292.40	292.65	293.90	298.20	294.80	293.10	305.80	301.80	301.35
Feed handling & management charge	21.00	21.00	21.00	21.00	21.00	21.00	21.00	21.00	21.00	21.00
Vet medicine	3.00	3.00	3.00	3.00	3.00	3.00	3.00	3.00	3.00	3.00
Interest on feeder & 1/2 feed	31.95	31.94	33.69	35.34	35.95	36.22	36.03	38.04	37.45	37.15
Death loss (1.5 percent of purchase)	5.19	5.18	5.58	5.95	6.06	6.15	6.12	5.86	5.48	5.43
Marketing[2]	f.o.b.	f.o.b.	f.o.b.	f.o.b.	f.o.b.	f.o.b.	f.o.b.	f.o.b.	f.o.b.	f.o.b.
Total	704.98	705.72	734.88	762.87	762.87	777.99	774.03	771.13	741.33	736.56
Selling price required to cover:[3]										
Feed and feeder costs (1,056 lb) $/cwt	60.31	60.38	62.94	65.40	66.49	66.73	66.38	65.94	63.20	62.79
All costs $/cwt	66.76	66.83	69.59	72.24	73.40	73.67	73.30	73.02	70.20	69.75
Selling price $/cwt[4]	71.00	70.09	67.31	65.31						
Net margin $/cwt	+4.24	+3.26	−2.28	−6.93						
Cost per 100-lb gain										
Variable costs less interest $/cwt	63.95	64.32	64.45	64.77	65.65	64.99	64.64	67.13	66.26	66.16
Feed costs $/cwt	58.11	58.48	58.53	58.78	59.64	58.96	58.62	61.16	60.36	60.27
Prices:										
Choice feeder steer 600-700 lb Amarillo $/cwt	57.72	57.54	62.00	66.12	67.32	68.31	67.97	65.08	60.94	60.28
Transportation rate $/cwt/100 miles[5]	.22	.22	.22	.22	.22	.22	.22	.22	.22	.22
Commission fee $/cwt	.50	.50	.50	.50	.50	.50	.50	.50	.50	.50
Milo $/cwt[6]	5.76	5.56	5.50	5.45	6.34	5.18	5.36	5.66	5.71	5.79
Corn $/cwt[5]	6.25	6.28	6.25	6.25	6.22	6.18	6.34	6.62	6.65	6.62
Cottonseed meal $/cwt[7]	14.50	15.50	15.50	16.00	17.00	16.00	16.00	16.00	15.50	15.00
Alfalfa hay $/ton[8]	131.00	132.00	136.00	136.00	142.00	151.00	134.00	144.00	136.00	138.00
Feed handling & management charge $/ton	10.00	10.00	10.00	10.00	10.00	10.00	10.00	10.00	10.00	10.00
Interest, annual rate	12.75	13.00	13.00	13.00	13.00	13.00	13.00	13.00	14.00	14.50

[1]Represents only what expenses would be if all selected items were paid for during the period indicated. The feed ration and expense items do not necessarily coincide with experience of individual feedlots. For individual use, adjust expenses and prices for management, production level, and locality of operation. Steers are assumed to gain 500 lbs in 180 days at 2.8 lbs per day with feed conversion of 8.4 lbs per pound gain. Revisions have been made per annual Agricultural Prices. [2]Most cattle sold f.o.b. at the feedlot with 4- percent shrink. [3]Sale weight 1,056 lbs (1,100 lbs less 4-percent shrink). [4]Choice slaughter steers, 900-1100 lbs, Texas-New Mexico direct. [5]Converted from cents per mile for a 44,000-lb haul. [6]Texas Panhandle elevator price plus $0.15/cwt handling and transportation to feedlots. [7]Average prices paid by farmers in Texas. [8]Average price received by farmers in Texas plus $30/ton handling and transportation to feedlots.

Table 11.—Corn Belt cattle feeding: Selected costs at current rates[1]

Purchased during Marketed during	Sept. 83 Mar.84	Oct. Apr.	Nov. May	Dec. June	Jan. 84 July	Feb. Aug.	Mar. Sept.	Apr. Oct.	May Nov.	June Dec.
					Dollars per head					
Expenses:										
600-lb feeder steer	349.86	361.20	366.00	381.90	390.36	398.70	404.52	405.06	394.20	376.20
Transportation to feedlot (400 miles)	5.28	5.28	5.28	5.28	5.28	5.28	5.28	5.28	5.28	5.28
Corn (45 bu)	147.60	139.50	143.10	141.30	141.30	139.05	148.95	150.75	152.10	151.20
Silage (1.7 tons)	46.95	46.55	46.67	47.45	48.85	49.69	51.28	51.76	52.01	50.30
Protein supplement (270 lb)	38.61	38.75	38.61	38.88	39.56	37.26	36.86	36.59	36.18	35.64
Hay (400 lb)	13.60	14.40	14.00	14.80	15.80	16.70	16.50	16.60	16.60	15.50
Labor (4 hours)	15.20	15.20	15.20	15.20	15.72	15.72	15.72	15.72	15.72	15.72
Management[2]	7.60	7.60	7.60	7.60	7.86	7.86	7.86	7.86	7.86	7.86
Vet medicine[3]	5.23	5.22	5.25	5.26	5.30	5.32	5.32	5.36	5.36	5.35
Interest on purchase (6 months)	23.60	24.74	25.07	26.16	26.64	27.21	27.61	28.01	27.26	26.01
Power, equip., fuel, shelter, depreciation[3]	24.38	24.33	24.46	24.53	24.73	24.81	24.94	24.99	24.99	24.97
Death loss (1% of purchase)	3.50	3.61	3.66	3.82	3.90	3.99	4.05	4.05	3.94	3.76
Transportation (100 miles)	2.31	2.31	2.31	2.31	2.31	2.31	2.31	2.31	2.31	2.31
Marketing expenses	3.35	3.35	3.35	3.35	3.35	3.35	3.35	3.35	3.35	3.35
Miscellaneous & indirect costs[3]	10.54	10.52	10.58	10.61	10.69	10.73	10.79	10.81	10.81	10.80
Total	697.60	702.56	711.13	728.44	741.65	747.88	765.36	768.49	757.97	735.25
Selling price required to cover:										
Feed and feeder costs (1,050 lb) $/cwt	56.82	57.18	57.94	59.46	60.56	61.09	62.68	62.93	62.01	59.89
Selling price required to cover all costs (1,050 lb) $/cwt	66.44	66.91	67.73	69.38	70.63	71.24	72.89	73.19	72.19	69.93
Feed costs per 100-lb gain $/cwt	54.84	53.15	53.86	53.87	54.56	53.93	56.35	56.82	57.09	56.14
Choice steers, Omaha $/cwt	68.60	67.86	65.89	64.28						
Net margin $/cwt	+2.16	+0.95	−1.84	−5.10						
Prices:										
Feeder steer, Choice (600-700 lb) Kansas City $/cwt	58.31	60.20	61.00	63.65	65.06	66.45	67.42	67.51	65.70	62.70
Corn $/bu[4]	3.28	3.10	3.18	3.14	3.14	3.09	3.31	3.35	3.38	3.96
Hay $/ton[4]	68.00	72.00	70.00	74.00	79.00	83.50	82.50	83.00	83.00	77.50
Corn silage $/ton[5]	27.62	27.38	27.45	27.91	28.74	29.23	30.16	30.45	30.60	29.59
32-36% protein supp. $/cwt[6]	14.30	14.35	14.30	14.40	14.65	13.80	13.65	13.55	13.40	13.20
Farm labor $/hour	3.80	3.80	3.80	3.80	3.93	3.93	3.93	3.93	3.93	3.93
Interest rate, annual	13.49	13.70	13.70	13.70	13.65	13.65	13.65	13.83	13.83	13.83
Transportation rate $/cwt per 100 miles[7]	.22	.22	.22	.22	.22	.22	.22	.22	.22	.22
Marketing expenses $/cwt[8]	3.35	3.35	3.35	3.35	3.35	3.35	3.35	3.35	3.35	3.35
Index of prices paid by farmers (1910-14=100)	1112	1110	1116	1119	1128	1132	1138	1140	1140	1139

[1]Represents only what expenses would be if all selected items were paid for during the period indicated. The feed ration and expense items do not necessarily coincide with experience of individuals for management, production level, and locality of operation. Revisions have been made per annual Agricultural Prices. [2]Assumes 1 hour at twice the labor rate. [3]Adjusted monthly by the index of prices paid by farmers for commodities, services, interest, taxes, and wage rates. [4]Average price received by farmers in Iowa and Illinois. [5]Corn silage price derived from an equivalent price of 5 bushels corn and 330 lb hay. [6]Average price paid by farmers in Iowa and Illinois. [7]Converted from cents/mile for a 44,000-pound haul. [8]Yardage plus commission fees at a Midwest terminal market.

Table 12.—July 1 feeder cattle supply

Item	1980	1981	1982	1983	1984	1984/83
			1,000 head			% change
Calves, 500 lb[1]						
On farms	35,862	36,549	36,650	35,970	35,500	1.3
On fe [2]	390	264	328	286	344	+20.3
Total	35,472	36,285	36,322	35,684	35,156	-1.5
Steers & heifers, 500 + lb[3]						
On farms	24,193	23,748	23,990	24,730	24,450	-1.1
On feed[2]	9,614	9,685	10,198	10,312	9,812	-4.8
Total	14,579	14,063	13,792	14,418	14,638	+1.5
Total supply	50,051	50,348	50,114	50,102	49,794	-0.6

[1]Less than. [2]Estimated U.S. steers and heifers. [3]Not including heifers for cow replacement.

Table 13.—Feeder steer prices consistent with breakeven, given corn and fed steer prices[1]

Corn	Choice steers, $/cwt				
	55	60	65	70	75
$/bu	Feeder steers, $/cwt				
2.50	43.5	52.5	61.5	70.0	79.0
2.75	41.5	50.5	59.0	68.0	76.5
3.00	39.5	48.0	57.0	66.0	74.5
3.25	37.0	46.5	55.0	63.5	72.5
3.50	35.0	44.0	52.5	61.5	70.5

[1]Assuming all other costs at June 1984 levels. Assumes milo equals 92 percent of the corn feeding value. (See Great Plains custom cattle feeding table.)

Second-Quarter Veal Production Up 15 Percent

Commercial slaughter of calves rose 11 percent from a year earlier during the second quarter. Commercial production for the quarter, at 113 million pounds, was up 15 percent from last year. First-half 1984 production increased 14 percent over a year earlier.

Table 14.—Commercial calf slaughter and production

Year	Slaughter[1]	Average dressed weight	Production[1]
	1,000 head	Lb	Million lb
1982:			
I	770	139	107
II	675	147	99
III	770	139	107
IV	806	136	110
Year	3,021	140	423
1983:			
I	734	140	103
II	669	146	98
III	805	137	110
IV	868	135	117
Year	3,076	139	428
1984:[2]			
I	817	141	115
II	745	152	113

[1]May not add due to rounding. [2]Preliminary.

The average price of Choice vealers at South St. Paul was $75.47 per cwt for June and $77 for the second quarter. Prices began to fall off during July, averaging $67.50 the first week.

Calf slaughter will likely decline through the second half as cattle feeding activity picks up, and it will probably show a 10- to 15-percent decrease during 1985. Commercial veal production during first-half 1985 may decline 15 to 20 percent from the first half this year. For all of 1985, veal output will probably drop 8 to 12 percent.

Hogs

Hog prices in the mid-$50's per cwt and moderating feed costs have recently raised farrow-to-finish producers' returns above total costs for the first time in over a year. Weekly hog prices averaged $48-$49 per cwt from late March through late June, then rose quickly to $54-$55 in July. Meanwhile, July corn prices softened about 15 cents a bushel from June, and soybean meal prices dropped about $16 a ton. However, feed costs remain relatively high. Thus, tight credit conditions and some uncertainty about the 1984 corn crop may discourage producers from expanding the breeding herd until this fall.

Pork Production To Decline; Prices Higher

Commercial hog slaughter in second-half 1984 is forecast to be 11 percent below last year, and slightly lower than suggested by the June 1 market hog inventory. Last summer, producers began liquidating the breeding herd. This year, in contrast, they are expected to hold the breeding herd steady this summer and possibly begin expanding this fall. Live hog imports from Canada are expected to be well above 1983 levels, adding to slaughter. Second-half slaughter may also be augmented by a slight increase in the average dressed weight, especially if feed costs decline further. Still, production is forecast to be 11 percent below last year. For all of 1984, commercial production is expected to total 14.4 billion pounds, down 5 percent from last year. Commercial slaughter may total about 83.5 million head, also down 5 percent.

Expected lower pork and beef production, along with a strong economy, will boost hog prices this summer and fall. However, burdensome frozen pork stocks and rising

11

year-over-year broiler production will be price-weakening factors. Hog prices in the second half are expected to average $52 to $56 per cwt, compared with $45 last year.

Table 15.—Federally inspected hog slaughter

Week ended	1982	1983	1984
		Thousands	
Jan. 1[1]	1,428	1,204	1,350
8	1,881	1,487	1,418
15	1,656	1,564	1,708
22	1,643	1,561	1,625
29	1,623	1,531	1,577
Feb. 5	1,552	1,353	1,543
12	1,650	1,467	1,571
19	1,484	1,492	1,578
26	1,652	1,449	1,579
Mar. 5	1,698	1,544	1,656
12	1,676	1,646	1,791
19	1,663	1,584	1,691
26	1,705	1,550	1,681
Apr. 2	1,609	1,573	1,695
9	1,606	1,620	1,695
16	1,608	1,759	1,728
23	1,656	1,724	1,642
30	1,640	1,714	1,588
May. 7	1,596	1,680	1,635
14	1,610	1,663	1,664
21	1,553	1,637	1,579
28	1,532	1,580	1,578
June 4	1,279	1,409	1,367
11	1,561	1,641	1,591
18	1,467	1,550	1,541
25	1,416	1,532	1,431
July 2	1,394	1,592	1,438
9	1,162	1,370	1,105
16	1,434	1,581	
23	1,352	1,515	
30	1,357	1,558	
Aug. 6	1,398	1,497	
13	1,391	1,566	
20	1,424	1,554	
27	1,400	1,526	
Sept. 3	1,411	1,613	
10	1,286	1,435	
17	1,527	1,772	
24	1,418	1,716	
Oct. 1	1,501	1,732	
8	1,482	1,841	
15	1,536	1,844	
22	1,599	1,895	
29	1,614	1,844	
Nov. 5	1,620	1,927	
12	1,677	1,955	
19	1,650	1,981	
26	1,310	1,593	
Dec. 3	1,676	1,994	
10	1,523	1,941	
17	1,588	1,804	
24	1,278	1,465	

[1]Corresponding dates-1982: January 2, 1982; 1983: January 1, 1983; 1984: December 31, 1983.

Feeding Margins
Turn Sharply Negative

Hog feeding margins turned sharply negative in the second quarter, after being near breakeven in the first quarter. The negative feeding margins, combined with prospects for continued high feed costs through at least early fall and lower-than-expected hog prices this summer, have depressed feeder pig prices. Prices for 40- to 50-pound No. 1 and 2 feeder pigs in Southern Missouri averaged about $34 per head in July, down $17 from April. However, the recent rise in hog prices, together with some recent moderation in feed costs should boost feeder pig prices. Feeder pig prices may average in the high $30's to low $40's this summer and rise to the mid-to-high $40's in the fall, especially if corn prices drop sharply.

Frozen Pork Stocks
Highest Since 1971

Despite a 7-percent drop from May, frozen pork stocks on June 30 totaled 406 million pounds, up 45 percent from a year earlier and the highest since 1971. Frozen pork bellies totaled 115 million pounds, up 81 percent from a year earlier and also the highest since 1971. Frozen hams totaled 74 million pounds, up 89 percent from last year.

Pork Production To Decline;
Prices To Increase

The June 1 farrowing intentions indicate that pork production may continue to decline through first-half 1985. Producers in the 10 quarterly reporting States indicated they intend to have 8 percent fewer sows farrow during June-August than a year earlier and 7 percent fewer in September-November. During February-April, the breeding period for sows farrowing during June-August, hog prices averaged $47 per cwt and the average farm price of corn was $3.21 a bushel. So, producers will likely carry through with their June-August intentions.

The breeding season for the September-November pig crop is May-July. In May-July, hog prices averaged about $51 per cwt and the farm price of corn about $3.34 a bushel. So, during the breeding season, producers' returns were still below total costs. In addition, the tight financial situation may have encouraged some producers to sell gilts to help reduce debt or raise money for current operating expenses. Thus, producers will likely also carry through their intentions to reduce sow farrowings during September-November by 7 percent or more.

Commercial pork production in first-quarter 1985 is projected at 3.45 million pounds, down 8 percent from a year earlier. Commercial slaughter may be 7 to 9 percent below 1984's 21.8 million head. If a large corn crop is realized, producers may be adding gilts to the breeding herd during the quarter, rather than reducing breeding stock, as was the case in 1984. With lower corn prices, producers are expected to feed barrows and gilts to heavier weights. Thus, the average dressed weight may be slightly higher than this year's 171 pounds.

Table 16.—Commercial hog slaughter[1] and production

Year	Barrows and gilts	Sows	Boars	Total[2]	Average dressed weight	Commercial production[2]
		1,000 head			*Lb*	*Mil. lb*
1982:						
I	20,347	1,093	274	21,714	170	3,693
II	19,498	956	258	20,712	171	3,550
III	17,668	1,030	242	18,940	171	3,240
IV	19,583	1,023	219	20,825	175	3,638
Year	77,096	4,102	993	82,191	172	14,121
1983:						
I	19,141	852	219	20,212	172	3,483
II	20,367	1,053	246	21,666	174	3,771
III	19,648	1,450	274	21,372	171	3,657
IV	22,808	1,291	235	24,334	173	4,206
Year	81,964	4,646	974	87,584	173	15,117
1984:[3]						
I	20,545	1,023	234	21,802	171	3,737
II	19,882	989	249	21,120	174	3,670

[1]Classes estimated. [2]Totals may not add due to rounding. [3]Preliminary.

Table 17.—Corn Belt hog feeding: Selected costs at current rates[1]

Purchased during / Marketed during	Sept. 83 Jan. 84	Oct. Feb.	Nov. Mar.	Dec. Apr.	Jan. 84 May	Feb. June	Mar. July	Apr. Aug.	May Sept.	June Oct.
				Dollars per head						
Expenses:										
40-lb feeder pig	22.96	22.27	24.54	27.65	33.61	43.48	50.12	51.08	42.85	39.48
Corn (11 bu)	36.08	34.10	34.98	34.54	34.54	33.99	36.41	36.85	37.18	36.96
Protein supplement (130 lb)	22.75	22.04	22.30	22.04	22.10	21.19	20.93	20.61	20.41	20.15
Labor & management (1.3 hr)	10.48	10.48	10.48	10.48	10.83	10.83	10.83	10.83	10.83	10.83
Vet medicine[2]	2.64	2.63	2.64	2.65	2.67	2.68	2.70	2.70	2.70	2.70
Interest on purchase (4 months)	1.03	1.02	1.12	1.26	1.53	1.98	2.28	2.35	1.98	1.82
Power, equip., fuel, shelter, depreciation[2]	6.41	6.39	6.43	6.45	6.50	6.52	6.55	6.57	6.57	6.56
Death loss (4% of purchase)	.92	.89	.98	1.11	.1.34	1.74	2.00	2.04	1.71	1.58
Transportation (100 miles)	.48	.48	.48	.48	.48	.48	.48	.48	.48	.48
Marketing expenses	1.14	1.14	1.14	1.14	1.14	1.14	1.14	1.14	1.14	1.14
Miscell. & indirect costs[2]	.66	.65	.66	.66	.67	.67	.67	.67	.67	.67
Total	105.54	102.09	105.75	108.45	115.41	124.70	134.12	135.32	126.52	122.37
Selling price/cwt required to cover:										
Feed and feeder costs (220 lb) $/cwt	37.18	35.64	37.19	38.28	41.02	44.85	48.85	49.33	45.65	43.90
Selling price/cwt required to cover all costs (220 lb) $/cwt	47.97	46.40	48.07	49.30	52.46	56.68	60.96	61.51	57.51	55.62
Feed cost per 100-lb gain (180 lb) $/cwt	32.68	31.19	31.82	31.43	31.47	30.66	31.86	31.92	31.99	31.73
Barrows and gilts 7 markets $/cwt	49.91	46.31	46.83	48.30	48.06	50.36				
Net margin $/cwt	+1.94	−0.09	−1.24	−1.00	−4.40	−6.32				
Prices:										
40-lb feeder pig (So. Missouri) $/head	22.96	22.27	24.54	27.65	33.61	43.48	50.12	51.08	42.85	39.48
Corn $/bu[3]	3.28	3.10	3.18	3.14	3.14	3.09	3.31	3.35	3.38	3.36
38-42% protein supp. $/cwt[4]	17.50	16.95	17.15	16.95	17.00	16.30	16.10	15.85	15.70	15.50
Labor & management $/hr[5]	8.06	8.06	8.06	8.06	8.33	8.33	8.33	8.33	8.33	8.33
Interest rate (annual)	13.49	13.70	13.70	13.70	13.65	13.65	13.65	13.83	13.83	13.83
Transportation rate $/cwt (100 miles)[6]	.22	.22	.22	.22	.22	.22	.22	.22	.22	.22
Marketing expenses $/cwt[7]	1.14	1.14	1.14	1.14	1.14	1.14	1.14	1.14	1.14	1.14
Index of prices paid by farmers (1910-14=100)	1112	1110	1116	1119	1128	1132	1138	1140	1140	1139

[1]Although a majority of hog feeding operations in the Corn Belt are from farrow to finish, relative fattening expenses will be similar. Costs represent only what expenses would be if all selected items were paid for during the period indicated. The feed rations and expense items do not necessarily coincide with the experience of individual feeders. For individual use, adjust expenses and prices for management, production level, and locality of operation. Revisions have been made per annual Agricultural Prices. [2]Adjusted monthly by the index of prices paid by farmers for commodities, services, interest, taxes, and wage rates. [3]Average price received by farmers in Iowa and Illinois. [4]Average prices paid by farmers in Iowa and Illinois. [5]Assumes an owner-operator receiving twice the farm labor rate. [6]Converted from cents/mile for a 44,000-pound haul. [7]Yardage plus commission fees at a Midwest terminal market.

13

Production in second-quarter 1985 is projected at 3.4 million pounds, down 7 percent from a year earlier. Slaughter is likely to be 5 to 7 percent below the 21.1 million head slaughtered in 1984. The average dressed weight may decline 1 to 3 pounds from this year's 174 pounds, as producers market hogs in a normal pattern rather than holding them for an expected price increase.

For all of 1985, commercial production may total about 14.1 billion pounds, depending on when the expansion in breeding herds occurs. Current expectations are that the fourth-quarter will be the only quarter in 1985 to show a year-over-year increase in production. The actual expansion will depend largely, as usual, on hog-corn price relationships in the coming months.

Hog prices in first-half 1985 are expected to average $56 to $60 per cwt. Moderately lower beef production and a continuing strong economy will be price-strengthening factors, but rising broiler production will be a price-weakening influence. For the year, hog prices may average $55 to $61 per cwt, up from the $50 to $52 projected for 1984.

Sheep and Lambs

Although lamb and mutton production in first-half 1984 rose 5 percent over a year earlier, Choice slaughter lamb prices averaged slightly higher than a year before and feeder lamb prices averaged about the same. However, because of flock reductions—largely induced by poor range conditions, especially in the Edwards Plateau area of Texas—mature sheep prices averaged nearly $2 per cwt below last year. Higher feed costs and moderate increases in other expenses have pushed up the cost of production, but higher wool prices and wool incentive payments may offset some of the increase.

Table 16.—Commercial sheep and lamb slaughter[1] and production

Year	Lambs and yearlings	Mature sheep	Total[2]	Average dressed weight	Commercial production[2]
	1,000 head			*Lb*	*Million lb*
1982:					
I	1,521	81	1,602	56	90
II	1,406	131	1,537	55	85
III	1,500	128	1,628	54	88
IV	1,555	127	1,681	55	93
Year	5,982	467	6,449	55	356
1983:					
I	1,533	91	1,624	57	93
II	1,441	135	1,576	56	89
III	1,597	142	1,739	54	94
IV	1,555	125	1,680	54	91
Year	6,126	493	6,619	55	367
1984:[3]					
I	1,611	104	1,715	57	98
II	1,544	162	1,706	54	92

[1]Class estimated. [2]May not add due to rounding. [3]Preliminary.

Commercial lamb and mutton production in the third quarter is forecast to total 85 million pounds, down 10 percent from a year earlier. Although lamb and sheep slaughter during the first 4 weeks in July was down about 3 percent from a year ago, a sharp year-over-year reduction is expected for the remainder of the quarter. Some lambs were marketed early this year because of poor forage conditions and some flock rebuilding is expected, especially in States hit by extreme cold weather this spring. In the fourth quarter, commercial lamb and mutton production is forecast to total 80 million pounds, down 12 percent from a year earlier.

Choice lamb prices at San Angelo averaged about $60 per cwt in July and may average $60 to $63 in the third quarter, which normally sees the lowest prices. In the fall, prices may rise seasonally and average $61 to $65.

For all of 1984, commercial lamb and sheep slaughter may total about 6.45 million head, down 2 percent from 1983. The January 1, 1984, inventory of all sheep and lambs was down 5 percent from last year. Because of extreme weather and poor forage conditions, the 1984 lambing rate (lambs per 100 ewes 1 year and older) is expected to be below 1983's 99 lambs—perhaps 92-95. If this lambing rate is realized, the 1984 lamb crop will be 9 to 13 percent below last year. This lower lamb crop, together with other indicators, suggests that the inventory of sheep and lambs may be around 10 million head on January 1, 1985, down 8 to 10 percent from a year earlier.

Commercial lamb and mutton production in first-quarter 1985 may total 85 million pounds, down 13 percent from a year earlier. In this quarter, slaughter will be drawn largely from 1984-crop lambs on feed on January 1, 1985. Expected tighter feeder lamb supplies this fall suggest that the number of lambs on feed will be substantially below January 1, 1984. In addition, new-crop lambs in central California may not be marketed as early as they were in 1984.

Commercial lamb and mutton production in second-quarter 1985 may be 13 to 15 percent below this year. Lamb slaughter during the quarter comes largely from the remaining old-crop lambs on feed and new-crop lambs in California and Arizona.

Choice slaughter lamb prices at San Angelo may average $62 to $66 in first-quarter 1985, then rise seasonally to $64 to $68 in the second quarter. Higher prices in the red meat complex and a strong economy will be price-strengthening factors.

Table 19.—Selected price statistics for meat animals and meat

Item	1983				1984							
	Oct.	Nov.	Dec.	IV	Jan.	Feb.	Mar.	I	Apr.	May	June	II
	Dollars per cwt											
SLAUGHTER STEERS:												
Omaha:												
Choice, 900-1100 lb	59.58	59.41	62.85	60.61	67.08	67.07	68.60	67.58	67.86	65.89	64.28	66.01
Good, 900-1100 lb	55.20	54.55	57.15	55.63	59.68	60.11	62.48	60.76	61.36	59.34	58.34	59.68
California, Choice												
900-1100 lb	60.19	60.50	66.25	62.31	68.19	67.70	69.56	68.48	68.38	64.85	63.97	65.73
Colorado, Choice												
900-1100 lb	60.20	60.82	66.25	62.42	69.50	67.71	70.08	69.10	69.61	66.64	65.49	67.25
Texas, Choice												
900-1100 lb	60.71	61.31	67.16	63.06	69.49	68.43	71.00	69.64	70.09	67.31	65.31	67.57
SLAUGHTER HEIFERS:												
Omaha:												
Choice, 900-1100 lb	58.50	58.45	62.77	59.91	66.46	66.02	67.52	66.67	66.75	64.89	63.52	65.05
Good, 700-900 lb	53.66	53.55	57.32	54.84	59.41	59.07	61.49	59.99	60.28	59.14	58.40	59.27
COWS:												
Omaha:												
Commercial	37.98	34.68	34.16	35.61	34.70	40.47	44.31	39.83	43.85	42.79	42.91	43.18
Utility	37.42	34.14	33.58	35.05	33.26	39.69	44.01	38.99	42.88	42.17	42.16	42.40
Cutter	35.16	32.57	31.82	33.18	30.82	37.58	42.08	36.83	40.98	39.45	40.00	40.14
Canner	32.85	29.62	28.94	30.47	28.27	33.74	37.21	33.07	36.94	35.78	36.18	36.30
VEALERS:												
Choice, So. St. Paul	66.75	67.50	67.50	67.25	64.94	77.50	77.50	73.31	77.50	78.00	75.47	76.99
FEEDER STEERS:[1]												
Kansas City:												
Medium No. 1,												
400-500 lb	65.48	66.20	66.38	66.02	67.18	71.51	72.08	70.26	71.56	70.15	67.82	69.84
Medium No. 1,												
600-700 lb	60.20	61.00	63.65	61.62	65.06	66.45	67.42	66.31	67.51	65.70	62.70	65.30
All weights												
and grades	56.97	58.12	61.00	58.70	64.39	65.97	66.30	65.55	64.15	60.82	59.28	61.42
Amarillo:												
Medium No. 1,												
600-700 lb	57.54	62.00	66.12	61.89	67.32	68.31	67.97	67.87	65.08	60.94	60.28	62.10
Georgia auctions:												
Medium No. 1,												
600-700 lb	54.00	57.20	57.33	56.18	60.38	62.90	61.88	61.72	59.25	57.30	56.00	57.52
Medium No. 2,												
400-500 lb	53.88	57.90	58.33	56.70	58.38	62.40	60.62	60.47	59.00	56.60	55.00	56.87
FEEDER HEIFERS:												
Kansas City:												
Medium No. 1,												
400-500 lb	52.48	54.08	55.54	54.03	55.98	59.48	60.15	58.54	59.00	58.74	56.40	58.05
Medium No. 1,												
600-700 lb*	52.22	52.91	56.70	53.94	58.19	59.79	60.28	59.42	58.60	57.56	55.12	57.09
SLAUGHTER HOGS:												
Barrows and gilts:												
Omaha:												
No. 1 & 2,												
200-230 lb	42.18	40.16	49.19	43.84	50.88	47.15	47.94	48.66	49.13	48.50	51.53	49.72
All weights	41.65	38.65	46.03	42.11	49.79	46.28	47.07	47.71	48.31	47.77	49.75	48.61
Sioux City	41.64	38.81	46.53	42.33	50.14	46.68	47.36	48.06	48.69	48.22	50.04	48.98
7 markets[2]	41.38	38.79	46.37	42.18	49.91	46.31	46.83	47.68	48.30	48.06	50.36	48.91
Sows:												
7 markets[2]	36.76	32.95	38.53	36.08	44.97	44.27	45.66	44.97	46.03	43.95	43.45	44.48
FEEDER PIGS:												
No. 1 & 2, So.												
Mo., 40-50 lb												
(per hd.)	22.27	24.54	27.65	24.82	33.61	43.48	50.12	41.40	51.08	42.85	39.48	44.47

Continued—

15

Item	1983				1984							
	Oct.	Nov.	Dec.	IV	Jan.	Feb.	Mar.	I	Apr.	May	June	II ·
	Dollars per cwt											
SLAUGHTER LAMBS:												
Lambs, Choice, San Angelo	54.44	57.94	60.50	57.63	60.62	58.75	58.50	59.29	65.88	63.50	59.88	63.09
Lambs, Choice, So. St. Paul	53.85	54.50	57.62	55.32	56.60	56.82	57.50	56.97	61.55	61.42	58.85	60.61
Ewes, Good, San Angelo	13.13	17.17	18.33	16.21	20.00	30.40	22.88··	24.43	22.25	13.45	15.56	17.09
Ewes, Good, So. St. Paul	9.55	9.12	11.00	9.89	12.50	13.72	17.68	14.63	11.75	10.09	10.50	10.78
FEEDER LAMBS:												
Choice, San Angelo	49.81	57.69	60.00	55.83	59.50	60.15	60.00	59.88	65.75	57.00	53.12	58.62
Choice, So. St. Paul	46.60	50.15	52.05	49.60	55.20	58.10	55.20	56.17	53.75	52.50	52.50	52.92
FARM PRICES:												
Beef cattle	51.70	51.20	54.60	52.50	57.10	59.70	61.70	59.50	60.10	58.60	57.60	58.77
Calves	57.10	59.20	60.60	58.97	60.90	63.90	63.70	62.83	62.30	60.80	59.20	60.77
Hogs	40.40	37.50	44.80	40.90	48.50	45.40	45.80	46.57	47.50	47.20	49.00	47.90
Sheep	13.70	15.10	16.40	15.07	18.20	19.60	18.70	18.83	16.30	13.00	13.80	14.37
Lambs	50.90	55.80	57.10	54.60	60.00	59.20	58.20	59.13	60.60	59.50	57.50	59.20
MEAT PRICES:												
Wholesale:												
Central U.S. markets												
Steer beef, Choice, 600-700 lb	91.24	91.57	99.82	94.21	105.74	102.86	105.14	104.58	103.50	99.62	98.54	100.55
Heifer beef, Choice 500-600 lb	88.85	89.34	96.06	91.42	100.80	99.21	101.50	100.53	98.88	96.28	93.70	96.29
Cow beef, Canner and Cutter	71.54	67.99	70.41	69.98	70.63	79.45	83.62	77.90	80.51	75.85	76.25	77.54
Pork loins, 14-17 lb[4]	N.A.	N.A.	N.A.	N.A.	104.36	94.68	88.75	95.93	91.86	95.31	97.59	94.92
Pork bellies, 12-14 lb	49.10	50.86	54.59	51.52	65.03	54.68	56.04	58.58	58.28	57.38	67.12	60.93
Hams, skinned, 14-17 lb	73.66	77.26	88.11·	79.68	70.44	68.80	78.00	72.41	77.52	74.44	72.03	74.66
East Coast:												
Lamb, Choice and Prime, 35-45 lb	125.00	127.00	131.25	127.75	131.38	132.90	131.71	132.00	135.00	137.00	127.54	133.18
Lamb, Choice and Prime, 55-65 lb	125.00	127.00	131.25	127.75	131.25	126.50	123.38	127.04	130.00	128.73	127.50	128.74
West Coast:												
Steer beef, Choice, 600-700 lb	95.44	95.05	104.81	98.43	108.20	106.67	108.30	107.72	107.85	101.10	97.69	102.21
	Cents per lb											
Retail:												
Beef, Choice	231.8	231.1	230.3	231.1	239.3	243.9	244.6	242.6	244.8	241.9	239.7	242.1
Pork	162.3	159.0	158.1	159.8	162.2	162.9	159.4	161.5	159.8	158.6	159.9	159.4
	1967=100											
Price Indexes (BLS 1967=100):												
Retail meats	260.4	258.6	258.3	259.1	266.4	270.0	268.8	268.4	268.9	267.9	266.8	267.9
Beef and veal	266.2	265.7	266.0	266.0	274.9	280.9	279.9	278.6	280.8	278.3	274.2	277.8
Pork	246.4	241.1	240.3	242.6	250.8	250.6	248.6	250.0	247.7	248.0	250.5	248.7
Other meats	262.2	262.6	261.3	262.0	262.5	265.0	265.1	264.2	264.6	265.7	267.5	265.9
Poultry	199.6	201.7	209.8	203.7	217.5	225.5	223.2	222.1	222.3	218.0	219.6	220.0
LIVESTOCK-FEED RATIOS, OMAHA[3]												
Beef steer-corn	18.4	18.3	19.8	18.8	21.6	22.1	21.1	21.6	20.4	19.7	19.1	19.7
Hog-corn	12.9	11.9	14.5	13.1	16.0	15.3	14.5	15.3	14.5	14.3	14.8	14.5

[1]Reflects new feeder cattle grades. [2]St. Louis, N.S.Y., Kansas City, Omaha, Sioux City, So. St. Joseph, So. St. Paul, and Indianapolis. [3]Bushels of No. 2 yellow corn equivalent in value to 100 pounds live weight. [4]Prior to January 1984 prices are 8-14 pounds.

PECTED:

	2,994	8,992	2,951	2,836	2,954	8,741	2,728	3,169	3,062	8,959
	1,404	4,072	1,392	1,367	1,447	4,206	1,338	1,565	1,507	4,410
	807	2,572	777	789	830	2,396	729	861	843	2,433
	731	2,167	736	629	618	1,983	600	674	642	1,916
gs	52	180	47	51	59	157	61	70	69	200
	262	787	253	236	264	753	226	233	219	678
bs	536	1,626	540	548	586	1,674	592	558	500	1,650
	7,515	23,496	6,947	6,591	7,578	21,116	6,953	7,153	6,392	20,498

Percent

| ws | 5.4 | 5.3 | 5.4 | 4.7 | 4.1 | 4.7 | 4.3 | 4.5 | 5.3 | 4.7 |

Pounds

eight

	1,077	1,080	1,072	1,079	1,078	1,077	1,073	1,068	1,064	1,068
	206	208	218	223	218	220	225	237	241	234
bs	111	111	113	115	116	115	113	110	108	110
	244	244	242	241	240	241	243	245	247	245
sed weight:										
	628	634	623	632	634	629	628	630	628	629
	124	125	132	136	133	134	136	145	147	143
tton	55	55	56	58	58	57	57	55	54	55
	174	174	172	172	172	172	173	175	176	175
	1,876	5,681	1,830	1,785	1,864	5,479	1,708	1,989	1,917	5,614
	32	97	33	32	34	99	31	33	31	95
tton	30	89	30	32	34	96	33	31	27	91
	1,301	4,069	1,194	1,129	1,301	3,624	1,200	1,246	1,123	3,569

1,000 head

	3,161	9,518	3,107	2,970	3,090	9,168	2,854	3,300	3,187	9,341
	284	868	277	255	285	817	249	255	242	746
ambs	551	1,680	553	561	600	1,715	616	574	517	1,707
	7,812	24,334	7,188	6,812	7,802	21,802	7,161	7,366	6,594	21,120

Million lbs

	1,965	5,962	1,913	1,858	1,937	5,708	1,776	2,059	1,984	5,819
	37	117	39	36	40	115	36	39	38	113
itton	30	91	31	32	35	98	34	31	27	92
	1,350	4,206	1,234	1,165	1,338	3,737	1,233	1,281	1,156	3,670

Million lbs

E STOCKS[1]
TER:[2, 3]

	325	325	338	332	326	326	325	313	304	304
	9	9	11	11	10	10	10	8	8	8
ton	11	11	8	8	8	8	9	9	9	9
	301	301	295	312	351	351	390	438	406	406
	646	646	652	663	695	695	734	768	727	727

ected and other commercial. [2]Beginning January 1977, excludes beef and pork stocks in cooler. [3]Stock levels end of quarter or

Table 21.—Selected foreign trade, by months

Item	1983						1984				
	July	Aug.	Sept.	Oct.	Nov.	Dec.	Jan.	Feb.	Mar.	Apr.	May
	Million lbs										
Imports (carcass weight):											
Beef	187.50	184.55	166.99	162.40	104.78	80.29	168.18	151.62	150.66	164.42	115.53
Veal	.66	.48	1.30	1.46	.67	.25	4.31	2.61	2.64	1.48	1.24
Pork	58.65	54.39	56.04	65.25	55.47	56.50	67.66	64.52	69.69	90.20	88.05
Lamb and mutton	2.35	1.08	2.56	.70	1.15	.71	.85	.44	1.90	3.25	1.66
Exports (carcass weight):											
Beef	19.45	25.57	26.60	28.94	26.62	16.15	26.58	26.96	36.50	25.28	24.95
Veal	.47	.33	.30	.38	.37	.10	.24	.43	.46	.27	.52
Pork	14.21	13.46	14.81	16.89	23.31	20.86	16.97	14.83	17.23	18.63	15.71
Lamb and mutton	.07	.11	.06	.16	.15	.14	.10	.21	.14	.14	.17
Shipments (carcass weight):											
Beef	3.04	2.77	3.33	3.16	3.83	3.48	2.98	4.32	3.51	3.97	4.20
Veal	.17	.12	.13	.05	.13	.14	.14	.09	.30	.06	.10
Pork	10.15	6.88	10.75	11.52	15.57	20.73	10.00	10.90	17.98	10.29	13.79
Lamb and mutton	.15	.11	.08	.13	.09	.07	.18	.04	.25	.10	.34
	Number										
Live animal imports:											
Cattle	74,665	81,733	59,418	28,514	36,636	130,014	128,019	116,603	97,858	63,313	48,801
Hogs	30,241	42,253	37,818	30,374	31,200	32,161	92,407	87,962	94,035	114,760	97,358
Sheep and lambs	2,443	3,070	693	65	278	43	444	490	20	9	27
Live animal exports:											
Cattle	3,719	4,910	4,428	3,818	7,058	5,966	3,561	3,012	2,218	3,873	6,330
Hogs	978	1,271	877	1,837	1,545	1,265	859	1,147	625	428	1,005
Sheep and lambs	25,377	26,101	18,629	13,320	28,416	21,916	25,770	15,075	24,208	35,206	17,506

Table 22.—Imports of feeder cattle, calves, and hogs from Canada and Mexico

Year and country	Jan.	Feb.	March	April	May	June	July	Aug.	Sept.	Oct.	Nov.	Dec.	Total
	Number												
1982													
Feeder cattle and calves													
Canada	21,482	22,123	47,488	59,974	55,570	35,666	26,099	30,687	36,790	42,952	66,601	41,338	486,770
Mexico	15,708	18,613	31,895	64,559	78,933	40,416	21,079	16,277	47,488	995	65,873	107,841	509,677
Hogs													
Canada	12,595	26,517	36,372	18,413	14,088	17,459	21,166	19,183	25,298	24,842	41,752	37,248	294,933
1983													
Feeder cattle and calves													
Canada	29,719	24,215	40,174	42,332	41,194	30,799	22,212	17,842	22,489	26,168	28,144	24,336	349,624
Mexico	31,523	22,411	21,664	15,741	81,320	122,502	51,981	63,347	36,417	1,994	8,004	104,761	561,665
Hogs													
Canada	68,538	34,033	40,956	39,764	27,222	32,905	30,241	42,253	37,818	30,374	31,200	32,087	447,391
1984													
Feeder cattle and calves													
Canada	13,812	22,425	20,074	35,117	34,211								
Mexico	113,941	93,891	70,948	27,318	14,051								
Hogs													
Canada	92,407	87,962	94,035	114,760	97,358								

POULTRY AND EGGS

Eggs

Production of eggs is increasing in 1984 and will likely continue growing through 1985. With supplies increasing, prices for eggs will remain relatively weak.

Even though producers sold more hens in June than last year, the number of layers on July 1 was up 3 percent. During the second quarter, the number of layers was above last year but the rate of lay was down. Egg production in April through June was 1,408 million dozen, nearly the same as in 1983.

Very favorable returns last fall and winter encouraged egg producers to order more replacement pullets, and these will enter the laying flock in second-half 1984. Productivity should increase during the remainder of 1984, climbing again to near last year's level. With additional pullets entering the flocks in the third quarter, egg output is expected to increase 2 percent from the 1,399 million dozen produced in 1983. During the fourth quarter, output may be 3 percent above 1983's 1,418 million dozen.

In July, wholesale prices were below the cost of production. If this continues, producers are likely to slow orders for replacement pullets for next year's flocks. However, the pullets added in second-half 1984 will continue

Table 23.—Layers on farms and eggs produced

Quarters	Number of layers		Eggs per layer		Eggs produced	
	1983	1984	1983	1984	1983	1984
	Million		Number		Million dozen	
I	282	277	61.1	60.6	1,432.9	1,401.1
II	273	277	61.9	61.0	1,405.2	1,408.2
III	271		62.1		1,399.2	
IV	276		61.6		1,418.6	
Annual	276		246.7		5,655.8	

Table 24.—U.S. egg exports to major importers, April-June 1983-1984 *

Country or area	1983	1984
	Thousand dozen	
Japan	12,381	2,421
Canada	2,157	2,229
Hong Kong	2,149	1,889
Trinidad-Tobago	1,002	712
Jamaica	642	670
Federal Rep. of Germany	1,068	267
Suriname	179	187
United Arab Emirates	67	166
Barbados	82	139
Trust Terr. of Pacific Is.	163	135
Bermuda	78	110
Haiti	71	99
France	8	85
Honduras	12	76
Colombia	185	74
Other	2,431	730
Total	22,673	9,988

* Shell and shell equivalent of egg products.

Table 25.—U.S. mature chicken exports to major importers, April-June 1983-1984

Country or area	1983	1984
	Thousand pounds	
Canada	2,211	3,150
Leeward-Windward Is.	2	849
Haiti	194	412
Trust Terr. of Pacific Is.	768	410
Mexico	88	335
Japan	77	243
Jamaica	0	216
Netherlands Antilles	170	185
Colombia	15	135
Hong Kong	21	95
Saudi Arabia	0	91
French Pacific Is.	56	35
Barbados	0	24
Turks & Caicos Islands	0	5
Bahamas	26	5
Other	208	5
Total	3,837	6,194

Table 26.—Shell eggs broken and egg products produced under Federal inspection, 1983-84

Period	Shell eggs broken	Egg products produced[1]		
		Liquid[2]	Frozen	Dried
	Thou. doz	Thou. lbs	Thou. lbs	Thou. lbs
1983				
January	57,526	38,965	23,822	6,369
February	56,439	35,217	22,792	5,801
March	61,229	40,626	25,564	6,368
April	52,493	37,566	22,516	5,753
May	61,369	42,366	25,310	7,738
June	71,820	47,408	30,099	10,476
July	64,019	41,293	26,139	9,814
August	72,163	51,671	26,341	9,038
September	66,689	48,597	26,064	6,421
October	64,397	45,201	26,649	6,830
November	55,635	38,216	24,962	5,994
December	48,142	33,472	23,299	4,974
1984				
January	52,102	40,207	22,669	4,522
February	62,797	45,962	27,413	6,878
March	64,036	46,404	30,206	7,022
April	55,214	40,168	25,232	4,947
May	68,536	49,138	28,464	6,968
June	67,724	48,829	27,737	6,543

[1]Includes ingredients added. [2]Liquid egg products produced for immediate consumption and for processing.

to increase production throughout 1985. During first-half 1985, egg output may be 3 percent above first-half 1984. The rate of increase may slow in second-half 1985 so that consumption in 1985 could be near the 1983 level. Per capita consumption would be leveling off, but down sharply from prior years.

Prices for eggs have been volatile in 1984. Any seasonal increase in demand, such as at Easter, greatly strengthened prices. During July, cartoned Grade A large eggs in New York averaged 71.5 cents per dozen, up from 68 cents last year, but down from the 83-cent average for the second quarter. Prices will likely strengthen seasonally as school resumes; in the third quarter they

19

may average 70 to 74 cents, down slightly from last year's 74. With production increasing in the fourth quarter, prices may average 68 to 72, down from 1983's 91 cents. During first-half 1985, prices are expected to average 60 to 68 cents, down from 93 this year. With production up only slightly in second-half 1985, prices then may average about the same as in second-half 1984.

Exports of shell eggs and egg products were 52 percent below last year in first-half 1984. Japan was our best customer, taking mainly egg products. Exports are expected to improve as domestic prices weaken and become competitive in more markets.

Table 27.—Egg-type chick hatchery operations

Month	Hatch			Eggs in incubator first of month		
	1982	1983	1984	1982	1983	1984
	Thousands			*Percent*		
January	36,652	32,630	36,806	98	86	112
February	36,413	32,956	37,699	103	86	112
March	44,220	39,281	45,136	99	81	125
April	46,626	36,663	47,227	94	79	127
May	47,342	38,330	48,781	102	76	131
June	39,424	37,487	46,516	98	91	128
July	35,405	30,530		107	86	125
August	33,455	30,929		98	97	
September	31,226	31,796		95	105	
October	32,345	32,343		95	100	
November	30,172	29,639		90	98	
December	31,140	34,351		90	112	

Table 28.—Force moltings and light-type hen slaughter, 1982-84

Month	Force molted layers[1]						Light-type hens slaughtered under Federal inspection[2]		
	Being molted			Molt completed					
	1982	1983	1984	1982	1983	1984	1982	1983	1984
	Percent						*Thousand*		
January	3.2		3.4	19.8		24.1	14,416	15,717	10,376
February	4.3	6.2	4.9	18.8	18.4	22.9	12,727	15,924	9,921
March	3.6	4.3	5.4	18.6	18.7	22.4	14,554	16,110	11,602
April		4.0	4.4		17.7	22.8	16,732	14,654	11,690
May		5.4	5.1		17.2	22.3	13,828	9,755	13,558
June	6.3	5.7	7.4	19.2	19.4	20.5	14,325	11,142	13,148
July		5.2	4.5		20.4	21.2	11,517	10,829	
August		4.6			22.1		14,111	11,820	
September	5.5	4.7		20.5	23.0		11,960	11,384	
October		5.0			23.6		11,797	10,139	
November		4.6			22.4		12,990	9,139	
December	3.3	2.3		18.2	24.9		16,101	10,080	

[1]Percent of hens and pullets of laying age in 17 selected States. [2]Revisions include data from late reports or other corrections developed by the Food Safety and Inspection Service.

Table 29.—Shell eggs: Supply and utilization, 1982-84[1]

Year	Stock change	Production	Hatching use	Eggs broken	Imports	Total supply	Exports and shipments	Military	Civilian Total	Per capita
									Million dozen										*Number*
198										
I	−.2	1,443.7	128.4	160.9	.5	1,154.7	29.2	5.4	1,120.0	58.6
II	.2	1,441.1	132.4	196.0	.2	1,113.2	16.5	4.6	1,092.2	57.0
III	.1	1,436.2	120.4	203.8	1.5	1,113.6	22.8	5.8	1,085.0	56.5
IV	−.2	1,478.6	124.5	172.0	.1	1,182.0	42.6	4.8	1,134.6	58.9
Year	0	5,799.5	505.6	732.7	2.3	4,563.4	111.1	20.5	4,431.8	231.1
1983[2]										
I	.5	1,432.9	128.4	175.2	5.0	1,134.8	15.5	5.5	1,113.8	57.7
II	−.8	1,405.2	129.2	185.7	2.8	1,092.4	13.3	6.3	1,072.7	55.5
III	.6	1,399.2	120.1	202.9	7.1	1,083.8	12.4	5.9	1,065.5	55.0
IV	.4	1,418.6	122.4	168.2	7.4	1,135.8	13.1	5.0	1,117.6	57.5
Year	.6	5,655.8	500.0	731.9	22.2	4,446.8	54.3	22.8	4,369.8	225.7
1984[2]										
I	−.7	1,401.1	132.8	178.9	12.4	1,101.2	9.5	3.9	1,087.6	55.8
II	−.2	1,408.2						4.6		

[1]Totals may not add because of rounding. [2]Preliminary.

Table 30.—Total eggs: Supply and utilization by quarters, 1982-84

Year	Production	Imports[1]	Beginning stocks[1]	Total supply	Ending stocks[1]	Exports and shipments[1]	Eggs used for hatching	Military[1]	Civilian Total	Per capita
									Million dozen									*Number[2]*
1982										
I	1,443.7	.5	17.5	1,447.2	14.4	53.1	128.4	5.9	1,259.8	65.9
II	1,441.1	.3	14.4	1,437.5	18.2	36.9	132.4	4.8	1,263.5	66.0
III	1,436.2	1.6	18.2	1,433.6	22.3	37.6	120.4	6.4	1,269.3	66.1
IV	1,478.6	.1	22.3	1,480.7	20.3	57.3	124.5	5.3	1,293.6	67.2
Year	5,799.5	2.5	17.5	5,799.1	20.3	184.9	505.6	22.4	5,086.1	265.2
1983[3]										
I	1,432.9	5.0	20.3	1,440.2	18.1	30.2	128.4	6.3	1,275.4	66.1
II	1,405.2	2.9	18.1	1,408.7	17.4	29.2	129.2	6.9	1,243.4	64.3
III	1,399.2	7.4	17.4	1,410.7	13.2	26.7	120.1	6.5	1,257.4	64.9
IV	1,418.6	8.2	13.2	1,430.7	17.6	26.4	122.4	5.4	1,276.6	65.7
Year	5,655.8	23.4	20.3	5,690.2	17.6	112.4	500.0	25.1	5,052.8	261.0
1984[3]										
I	1,401.1	13.9	9.3	1,414.3	10.2	17.5	132.8	4.2	1,259.6	64.7
II	1,408.2		10.2					5.3		

[1]Shell eggs and the approximate shell-egg equivalent of egg product. [2]Calculated from unrounded data. [3]Preliminary.

Table 31.—Egg prices and price spreads, 1983-84

Item	Jan.	Feb.	March	April	May	June	July	Aug.	Sept.	Oct.	Nov.	Dec.	Average
						Cents per dozen							
Farm price[1]													
1983	46.5	48.9	51.6	51.2	55.0	53.4	51.8	57.8	60.6	63.7	72.4	79.3	57.7
1984	92.8	88.8	73.5	87.4	62.3	53.8	52.8						
New York (cartoned)[2]													
Grade A, large													
1983	62.7	65.7	69.1	67.6	69.9	69.7	68.2	76.5	78.6	80.2	91.8	101.9	75.2
1984	115.0	104.0	91.0	103.7	75.9	70.7							
4-region average,													
Grade A, large													
Retail price													
1983	85.2	82.7	86.5	84.8	89.6	85.2	88.2	91.8	96.2	98.1	102.3	114.1	92.1
1984	130.8	133.2	117.1	120.9	108.1	91.5							
Price spreads													
Farm-to-consumer													
1983	41.8	36.1	35.0	35.3	35.7	32.3	37.2	32.0	34.1	34.1	25.7	26.9	33.9
1984	32.8	46.9	43.2	32.6	49.2	38.5							
Farm-to-retailer													
1983	21.2	18.9	18.2	19.0	17.7	16.2	18.9	17.4	17.2	17.3	14.1	14.0	17.5
1984	14.9	18.8	18.0	17.0	19.4	18.1							
Retail-to-consumer													
1983	20.6	17.2	16.8	16.3	18.0	16.1	18.3	14.6	16.9	16.8	11.6	12.9	16.3
1984	17.9	28.1	25.1	15.6	29.8	20.5							
						1967=100							
Consumer price index													
1983	172.9	169.3	175.0	174.9	181.8	173.8	177.9	183.7	193.3	200.1	208.2	234.0	187.1
1984	266.5	270.3	237.2	249.6	218.9	185.8							

[1]Market (table) eggs including eggs sold retail by the producer; data not available prior to 1982. [2]Price to volume buyers.

Broilers

Broiler output is likely to continue increasing through 1984 and 1985. Even with substantial increases in production, prices are likely to remain strong.

The output of young chicken meat from federally inspected slaughter plants totaled 3,331 million pounds in second-quarter 1984, up 55 million from 1983. The increase in output came from a gain in both numbers (up 8 million head from last year) and average weights (up 3 hundredth of a pound from last year). When producers are further processing birds, larger birds yield more high-priced breast meat. The demand for the more boneless breast meat, plus cool weather during much of the quarter, accounts for the slaughter weight increase. Hotter weather would reduce weights, but thus far summer temperatures have been below average.

Broiler producers have been increasing the number of eggs placed in incubators for third-quarter slaughter. Based on the hatch thus far and the eggs in incubators, output in the third quarter is expected to be up 5 percent from the 3.135 billion pounds produced last year. Slaughter of heavy hens has been trailing year-earlier numbers; producers have held their hens a few days longer to obtain hatching eggs to expand production. This has been necessary because the cumulative pullet chick placements 7 to 14 months ago were down from the previous year. Broiler production will likely decline seasonally in the fourth quarter from the third quarter and hatchery supply flocks will be able to provide the needed eggs. With supplies of red meats declining in the fourth quarter, broiler producers are expected to increase output about 6 percent from a year earlier.

Like egg producers, broiler producers have been adding more replacement pullets to the hatchery supply flock and consequently November and December will have cumulative placements above last year. With supplies of red meats not expected to increase until second-half 1985, broiler producers in the first half will likely expand production 5 to 6 percent above this year. With more red meat expected in the second half, broiler production may slow slightly and be well above this year's level.

Prices of whole broilers in the 12 cities during second-quarter 1984 averaged 56 cents per pound, up from 47 last year. With additional output of broilers but less competition from red meats, prices in the third quarter are expected to average 52 to 55 cents, near the 54 cents of 1983. In the fourth quarter, demand for broilers declines seasonally. Combined with an increase in output, this may pull average prices down to 50 to 54 cents, from 55 last year. In first-half 1985, prices may average 53 to 57 cents per pound, down from 59 this year. With more red meat in second-half 1985, broiler prices may average 50 to 55 cents, about the same as this year.

Exports of whole broilers and cut-up birds in the second quarter were 15 percent below last year's 113 million pounds. Japan was the largest market for U.S. broilers, and as in the past most sales were parts rather than whole birds. Exports in the fourth quarter may move slightly above last year if prices weaken. However, exports will still be very low relative to earlier years. Exports of broilers may decline even further in 1985.

Table 32.—Young chicken prices and price spreads, 1983-84

Item	Jan.	Feb.	March	April	May	June	July	Aug.	Sept.	Oct.	Nov.	Dec.	Average
						Cents per pound							
Farm price[1]													
1983	26.0	27.4	25.2	24.6	26.4	28.5	30.9	32.0	32.8	29.7	33.7	33.7	29.2
1984	36.9	37.4	37.8	34.8	33.5	33.2	35.5						
Wholesale RTC 9-city average[2]													
1983	43.1	45.2	41.9	40.9	46.9	49.1	52.8	54.2	54.5	50.4	56.3	57.1	49.4
1984	62.1	61.2	62.0	56.0	57.6	55.5	58.4						
4-region average retail price													
1983	69.2	70.4	70.3	67.9	69.1	70.3	72.8	74.0	77.0	73.8	76.9	81.4	72.8
1984	84.1	87.1	85.2	84.8	81.6	82.2							
Price spreads Farm-to-consumer													
1983	34.4	33.5	36.5	34.9	33.8	30.2	30.2	30.9	33.5	33.8	31.7	35.0	33.2
1984	34.2	37.0	35.0	43.9	36.6	37.6							
Farm-to-retailer													
1983	16.3	16.0	16.9	15.8	16.8	15.1	18.0	16.7	16.6	17.4	16.7	15.2	16.5
1984	17.7	17.9	16.6	21.4	17.2	17.1							
Retail-to-consumer													
1983	18.1	17.5	19.6	19.1	17.0	15.1	12.2	14.2	16.9	16.4	15.0	19.8	16.7
1984	16.5	19.2	18.3	22.4	19.4	20.5							
						1967 = 100							
Retail price index Whole chickens													
1983	186.8	190.6	190.7	184.5	187.7	192.1	198.7	202.1	209.6	199.1	207.6	219.4	197.4
1984	228.7	235.9	232.6	231.2	223.2	223.7							

[1]Live weight. [2]Beginning May 1983, 12-city composite weighted average.

Table 33.—Broiler chicks hatched and pullet chicks placed in hatchery supply flocks

Month	Broiler-type chicks			Pullet chicks placed in broiler hatchery supply flocks					
				Monthly placements			Cumulative placements 7-14 months earlier*		
	1982	1983*	1984	1982	1983	1984	1983	1984	1985
	Million			*Thousands*			*Thousands*		
January	372,503	382,604	370,024	3,379	3,169	3,202	27,265	26,428	27,277
February	336,484	348,287	356,386	3,152	3,310	2,977	27,179	25,349	
March	390,918	399,748	397,942	3,676	3,299	3,451	26,875	25,441	
April	385,801	388,781	394,842	3,640	3,143	4,012	26,359	25,169	
May	402,754	395,460	408,567	3,698	3,541	3,520	26,483	24,873	
June	385,164	382,189	397,071	2,934	3,147	3,399	26,371	24,700	
July	381,979	377,988		3,035	2,485		25,986	25,147	
August	377,760	372,246		3,361	3,347		25,457	24,808	
September	348,090	343,634		2,863	2,897		25,833	24,638	
October	344,579	345,253		3,276	3,014		26,097	25,604	
November	345,602	335,928		3,564	3,126		25,879	26,269	
December	373,949	374,881		3,255	3,590		26,557	26,892	

* = Revised.

Period[2]	Eggs set			Chicks placed		
	1982/83	1983/84	Percent of previous year	1982/83	1983/84	Percent of previous year
	Thousands		Percent	Thousands		Percent
November						
19	101,021	99,303	98	79,826	74,021	93
26	100,644	99,800	99	80,372	78,415	98
December						
3	97,509	100,213	103	80,674	80,864	100
10	100,149	98,974	99	80,066	79,598	99
17	100,905	99,093	98	80,024	80,372	99
24	101,502	100,278	99	78,701	80,184	102
31	102,141	99,622		80,616	79,519	99
January						
7	101,762	99,740	97	81,633	79,254	97
14	101,782	99,118	98	82,002	80,849	99
21	99,885	100,493	101	82,537	79,995	97
28	101,945	101,413	100	82,110	77,985	95
February						
4	103,052	102,185	99	82,030	78,873	96
11	103,598	101,571	98	79,795	80,945	101
18	103,813	102,724	99	81,839	81,301	99
25	105,134	105,245	100	83,030	82,368	99
March						
3	105,702	106,529	101	83,951	81,929	98
10	105,235	106,474	101	84,203	82,882	98
17	105,873	106,825	101	85,470	85,385	100
24	103,188	106,411	103	85,976	86,169	100
31	105,043	107,985	103	86,070	86,202	100
April						
7	104,680	108,597	104	85,456	85,462	100
14	104,286	108,214	104	83,405	85,569	103
21	103,308	107,373	104	85,274	87,093	102
28	101,114	105,980	105	84,966	88,344	104
May						
5	102,881	108,775	106	84,837	87,429	103
12	101,793[1]	107,463	106	84,137	86,913	103
19	102,512	107,855	105	82,602	85,741	104
26	102,787	107,489	105	83,366	87,095	104
June						
2	102,528	108,920	106	83,343	86,941	104
9	103,493	108,617	105	83,491	86,979	104
16	101,977	108,276	106	83,540	87,393	105
23	99,380	104,926	106	83,819	87,917	105
30	95,280	100,692	106	84,486	87,878	104
July						
7	99,600	106,546	107	83,702	87,091	104
14	99,886	105,517	106	80,707	84,089	104
21	100,089	105,575	105	76,852	80,196	104
28	99,227			81,042		
August						
4	98,790			80,892		
11	99,956			79,960		
18	98,543			78,733		
25	97,417			78,042		
September						
1	92,809			79,096		
8	90,407			78,579		
15	85,182			77,477		
22	95,745			72,852		
29	96,039			71,959		
October						
6	92,106			67,918		
13	86,564			76,910		
20	86,757			77,286		
27	91,574			74,430		
November						
3	97,046			69,939		
10	100,214			70,260		

[1] Ala., Ark., Calif., Del., Fla., Ga., Md., Miss., N.C., Pa., S.C., Tex., Va., W. Va., La., Mo., Tenn., Oreg., and Wash. [2] Weeks in 1983/84 and corresponding weeks in 1982/83.

Table 35.—Estimated costs and returns, 1981-83[1]

| Year | Production costs | | Wholesale | | Net returns |
	Feed	Total	Total costs[2]	Price[3]	
Market eggs (cts/doz)					
1981					
I	37.8	54.1	75.1	72.7	−2.4
II	37.6	53.9	74.9	68.8	−6.1
III	36.0	52.3	73.3	72.9	−0.3
IV	30.8	47.1	68.1	78.1	10.1
Year[4]	35.5	51.8	72.8	73.2	0.4
1982					
I	30.5	46.0	67.0	78.9	11.8
II	31.5	47.0	68.1	67.0	−1.0
III	30.0	45.5	66.6	67.0	0.4
IV	27.1	42.6	63.7	67.5	3.8
Year[4]	29.7	45.2	66.3	70.1	3.8
1983					
I	29.7	47.2	67.7	66.4	−1.2
II	33.5	51.0	71.5	69.2	−2.3
III	35.6	53.1	73.6	75.3	1.7
IV	37.7	55.2	75.7	90.7	15.0
Year[4]	34.1	51.6	72.1	75.4	3.3
1984					
I	35.4	53.6	74.3	103.0	28.6
II	36.7	54.9	75.6	90.6	15.0
Broilers (cts/lb)					
1981					
I	21.3	29.9	53.4	49.3	−4.1
II	20.6	29.1	52.5	46.7	−5.9
III	20.3	28.8	52.0	47.0	−5.0
IV	17.9	26.4	48.9	42.1	−6.8
Year[4]	20.0	28.6	51.7	46.3	−5.4
1982					
I	16.8	25.0	47.0	44.8	−2.2
II	17.3	25.6	47.7	45.2	−2.6
III	17.3	25.6	47.7	44.4	−3.3
IV	15.0	23.3	44.6	41.6	−3.1
Year[4]	16.6	24.9	46.8	44.0	−2.8
1983					
I	16.2	24.7	47.7	43.4	−4.3
II	18.1	26.6	50.2	45.6	−4.6
III	19.0	27.5	51.4	53.9	2.4
IV	21.4	29.9	54.6	54.6	.0
Year[4]	18.6	27.1	51.0	49.3	−1.7
1984					
I	20.3	29.1	53.9	61.8	7.9
II	19.5	28.3	52.8	56.8	4.1
Turkeys (cts/lb)					
1981					
I	32.0	43.5	69.0	64.2	−4.8
II	30.8	42.4	67.6	67.9	0.3
III	30.7	42.3	67.4	66.5	−1.0
IV	28.6	40.1	64.7	58.6	−6.1
Year[4]	30.3	41.8	66.9	64.0	−2.8
1982					
I	24.2	36.0	59.8	57.0	−2.8
II	25.1	36.9	60.9	59.4	−1.5
III	25.5	37.3	61.4	67.0	5.6
IV	23.2	35.0	58.5	66.9	8.3
Year[4]	24.5	36.3	60.1	63.7	3.5

See footnotes at end of table.

Table 35.—Estimated costs and returns, 1981-83[1]
Continued

| Year | Production costs | | Wholesale | | Net returns |
	Feed	Total	Total costs[2]	Price[3]	
1983					
I	22.7	35.9	60.6	56.4	−4.2
II	24.9	38.1	63.3	59.0	−4.3
III	27.0	40.2	66.0	63.7	−2.3
IV	29.8	43.0	69.4	71.0	1.5
Year[4]	26.6	39.8	65.4	63.5	−2.0
1984					
I	29.9	43.5	70.5	70.3	−0.2
II	27.9	41.5	67.9	70.1	2.2

[1] Estimated by computerized formula. Costs are weighted by monthly production. [2] Based on farm cost converted to wholesale market value. [3] Wholesale prices used are the 13-metro area egg price, 9-city weighted average broiler price, and a weighted average of 8-16 lb. young hens and 24-26 lb. toms in New York, Chicago, and Los Angeles. [4] Weighted average.

Table 36.—Federally inspected young chicken slaughter

Quarter and year	Number	Average weight	Live weight	Certified RTC
	Million	Pounds	Million pounds	
1982				
I	983	4.03	3,961	2,888
II	1,047	4.05	4,239	3,109
III	1,065	4.00	4,265	3,130
IV	973	4.10	3,991	2,911
Year	4,068	4.04	16,456	12,039
1983				
I	1,022	4.10	4,186	3,061
II	1,084	4.13	4,473	3,276
III	1,062	4.00	4,254	3,135
IV	965	4.13	3,981	2,917
Year	4,133	4.09	16,984	12,389
1984				
I	1,015	4.16	4,225	3,082
II	1,092	4.16	4,549	3,331

Table 37.—U.S. young chicken exports to major importers, April-June 1983-1984

Country or area	1983	1984
	Thousand pounds	
Japan	34,075	27,597
Hong Kong	15,060	17,493
Singapore	12,573	10,731
Jamaica	12,797	8,896
Canada	5,895	7,496
Leeward-Windward Is.	7,451	5,334
Mexico	3,291	4,249
Netherlands Antilles	3,419	2,970
Saudi Arabia	1,354	1,586
French Pacific Is.	1,968	1,403
Barbados	1,403	1,325
Kuwait	484	831
Federal Rep. of Germany	1,247	624
Brunei	970	570
Trust Terr. of Pacific Is.	694	529
Other	10,507	4,524
Total	113,189	96,156

Turkeys

Relative to last year, turkey production will likely decline during the rest of 1984. With reduced production, prices may strengthen from last year.

Output of turkey meat from federally inspected plants during the second quarter totaled 585 million pounds, up 1 percent from last year. The average weight of turkeys slaughtered was up 1 percent, while the number of birds was down but not enough to lower output.

The number of poults placed for third-quarter slaughter suggests output will be down slightly from the 760 million pounds produced last year. While poult placement for fourth-quarter slaughter is still incomplete, poults placed in May and June and eggs in incubators on July 1 suggest that output may be down 1 to 3 percent from last year's 759 million pounds.

Turkey producers may sharply expand production in 1985, if

● prices strengthen in second-half 1984;

● holiday movement keeps stocks low; and

● feed prices moderate after harvest.

Production in first-half 1985 may increase 6 to 7 percent from this year. During the second half, production is expected to expand about 5 percent from 1984.

Stocks of frozen turkey on July 1 totaled 227 million pounds, down 29 million from last year. Whole turkey represented 94 percent of the decline. Stocks of turkey are now being increased, as expected, and should peak seasonally at the end of the third quarter to help meet the additional demand for holiday birds in the fourth quarter.

During second-quarter 1984, prices of 8- to 16-pound hen turkeys in New York averaged 67 cents per pound, up from 57 last year. Prices in the second quarter often decline as stocks have to be moved to accommodate the current year's production. With stocks relatively low this year, though, prices were nearly the same in the first and second quarters. During the third quarter, prices of young hen turkeys will likely be strengthened by reduced supplies and higher prices for red meats. Prices may average 70 to 74 cents per pound, 10 to 14 above third-quarter 1983. If supplies decline in the fourth quarter, prices could average 72 to 76 cents, up from 69 last year. During first-half 1985, prices may average 67 to 71, near this year's 67 cents. With continued large supplies of turkey and increasing supplies of red meats, prices in second-half 1985 may fall to the mid-60's, down slightly from this year.

In second-quarter 1984, exports of whole turkey and turkey parts were down 52 percent from last year's 11 million pounds. The Federal Republic of Germany continued as our best customer, purchasing mostly turkey parts. During the second half, exports of turkey are likely to trail last year because of reduced supplies and higher prices. In 1985, exports may improve slightly.

Table 38.—Turkey prices and price spreads, 1983-84

Item	Jan.	Feb.	March	April	May	June	July	Aug.	Sept.	Oct.	Nov.	Dec.	Average
						Cents per pound							
Farm price[1]													
1983	32.4	32.8	33.3	32.3	35.0	36.5	34.3	35.2	39.5	39.9	40.7	45.8	36.5
1984	46.6	41.3	41.6	43.3	42.7	42.5	44.0						
New York, hens 8-16 lbs.[2]													
1983	53.6	54.9	56.0	54.4	56.6	60.9	58.5	57.6	65.0	65.1	67.0	76.1	60.5
1984	72.2	64.7	66.1	67.0	66.8	67.0							
4-region average retail price													
1983	91.4	92.4	91.8	92.6	92.8	92.3	93.0	91.4	90.4	95.3	87.7	89.4	91.7
1984	92.8	94.4	95.6	94.3	97.3	99.1							
Price spreads Farm-to-consumer													
1983	53.0	52.9	51.5	52.9	50.7	46.9	50.0	49.2	41.0	45.7	36.0	28.7	46.5
1984	36.3	45.2	44.7	42.3	47.0	47.9							
Farm-to-retailer													
1983	23.0	22.0	22.0	22.9	21.7	23.4	24.4	25.5	21.0	21.4	20.8	19.7	22.3
1984	21.9	24.5	23.9	23.2	25.3	24.6							
Retail-to-consumer													
1983	30.0	30.9	29.5	30.0	29.0	23.5	25.6	23.7	20.0	24.3	15.2	9.0	24.2
1984	14.3	20.6	20.8	19.1	21.7	23.2							
						December 1977=100							
Consumer price index													
1983	126.3	127.7	126.6	127.2	125.4	125.3	126.0	125.7	122.9	126.0	120.6	122.3	125.1
1984	125.4	128.5	127.9	128.0	130.3	131.6							

[1]Live weight. [2]Wholesale, ready-to-cook.

Table 39.—Federally inspected turkey slaughter

Quarter and year	Number	Average weight	Live weight pounds [1]	Certified RTC
	Million	*Pounds*	*Million pounds*	
1982				
I	26.4	19.68	519.2	410.4
II	35.0	18.91	661.0	527.9
III	51.0	18.67	951.7	761.5
IV	48.0	19.85	953.2	759.1
Year	160.4	19.24	3,085.1	2,458.9
1983				
I	29.0	20.16	584.4	462.2
II	37.8	19.29	729.7	581.5
III	50.8	18.82	955.7	760.3
IV	47.4	20.12	952.8	759.0
Year	165.0	19.54	3,222.6	2,563.1
1984				
I	27.0	20.27	546.8	432.3
II	37.6	19.51	733.6	585.3

Table 40.—U.S. turkey exports to major importers April-June 1983-1984

Country or Area	1983	1984
	Thousands pounds	
Federal Rep. of Germany	2,004	983
Canada	409	562
Mexico	38	434
Japan	865	389
Trust Terr. of Pacific Is.	534	356
Republic of South Africa	675	350
Hong Kong	1,129	341
Saudi Arabia	389	285
Western Samoa	28	266
Venezuela	397	265
Kuwait	78	168
Bahamas	217	145
Barbados	36	97
Leeward-Windward Is.	74	94
Haiti	0	92
Other	3,863	362
Total	10,736	5,188

Table 41.—Turkey hatchery operations, 1982-84

Month	Turkeys placed [1]						Eggs in incubators first of month, changes from previous year					
	Light breeds [2]		Heavy breeds [3]		Total		Light breeds [2]		Heavy breeds [3]		Total	
	1982-83	1983-84	1982-83	1983-84	1982-83	1983-84	1982-83	1983-84	1982-83	1983-84	1982-83	1983-84
	Thousands						*Percent*					
September	180	171	7,849	7,915	8,029	8,086	−47	32	3	−4	1	−5
October	171	159	9,477	9,043	9,648	9,202	−53	−19	7	−9	5	−9
November	162	222	11,442	10,747	11,604	10,969	−68	24	19	−5	14	−5
December	589	230	11,544	12,246	12,133	12,476	−63	−66	4	0	−1	−3
January	589	(4)	13,306	(4)	13,895	14,038	−10	−27	−3	−5	2	−8
February	568	(4)	14,617	(4)	15,185	15,316	−32	(4)	5	(4)	3	−3
March	583	(4)	18,239	(4)	18,822	18,286	−23	(4)	1	(4)	0	−2
April	675	(4)	19,089	(4)	19,764	19,088	18	(4)	−2	(4)	−3	−5
May	651	(4)	20,234	(4)	20,885	21,129	−14	(4)	−2	(4)	−2	1
June	688	(4)	20,339	(4)	21,027	20,449	−4	(4)	0	(4)	−1	−2
July	742		18,491		19,233		−30	(4)	−1	(4)	−2	−8
August	591		11,987		12,578		−27		−7		−8	

[1] Excludes exported poults. Placed estimates should not be used to measure change from previous year. [2] Normal mature marketing weight under 12 pounds. [3] Normal mature marketing weight 12 pounds or over. [4] Breakdown by breeds not shown to avoid disclosing individual operations.

CONSUMPTION AND PRICES

First-Half Consumption Up

Consumption of red meat and poultry in first-half 1984 increased about 1 percent from a year earlier. Consumption of both beef and pork increased, with beef rising about 2 percent. Turkey consumption declined, and broiler consumption was unchanged.

Retail prices in the second quarter averaged slightly below a year earlier. The retail beef price fell from April through June because of large beef supplies. The composite retail beef price was $2.42 a pound in the spring, about the same as in the winter quarter but slightly lower than last year. Second-quarter retail prices for pork also declined through May, as supplies of competing meats increased. Retail pork prices in June averaged $1.60, increasing slightly from May. The composite retail pork price fell about 7 percent to $1.59 a pound in the second quarter. Hog prices will likely rise as production declines this summer resulting in higher retail prices from the low prices in the second quarter.

Beef Price Spreads Fall in June

Beef farm-to-retail price spreads fell in June following 2 months of increase. Although beef retail prices have dropped since April, prices for Choice fed cattle decreased at a faster rate. Since retail price changes typically lag changes in the farm price, the farm-to-retail price spread for beef rose from 97.1 cents a pound in March to 103.0 in June, 2 cents higher than a year before. The farm-to-retail price spread for pork continued to fall in June, going to 79.9 cents a pound—15 cents below a year earlier. Price spreads tightened in June because live hog prices increased faster than the retail price did.

27

Table 42.—Beef, Choice Yield Grade 3: Retail, carcass, and farm values, spreads, and farmers' share[1]

Year	Retail price[2]	Gross carcass value[3]	Carcass by-product allow-ance[4]	Net carcass value[5]	Gross farm value[6]	Farm by-product allow-ance[7]	Net farm value[8]	Farm-retail spread			Farmers' share[9]
								Total	Carcass-retail	Farm-carcass	
						Cents per lb					*Percent*
1979	226.3	153.3	2.8	150.5	163.4	22.6	140.8	85.5	75.8	9.7	62
1980	237.6	157.7	2.3	155.4	161.9	16.9	145.0	92.6	82.2	10.4	61
1981[10]	238.7	151.5	2.1	149.3	154.5	16.0	138.5	100.2	89.4	10.8	58
1982	242.5	152.8	2.1	150.7	155.5	15.0	140.5	102.0	91.8	10.2	58
1983	238.1	147.4	2.0	145.4	151.8	15.6	136.2	101.9	92.7	9.2	57
1983											
I	237.9	146.7	1.7	144.9	149.9	13.5	136.4	101.5	93.0	8.5	58
II	245.1	158.0	2.0	156.1	162.9	15.5	147.4	97.7	89.0	8.7	60
III	238.4	142.8	2.1	140.7	147.0	16.5	130.5	107.9	97.7	10.2	55
IV	231.1	142.0	2.0	140.0	147.4	16.8	130.7	100.4	91.1	9.3	57
1984											
I	242.6	157.2	2.8	154.3	164.5	18.5	146.0	96.6	88.3	8.3	60
II	242.1	151.2	3.1	148.1	159.8	19.8	140.0	102.1	94.0	8.1	58
1984											
Jan.	239.3	158.7	2.8	155.9	164.1	18.0	146.1	93.2	83.4	9.8	61
Feb.	243.9	154.8	2.7	152.1	162.8	18.3	144.5	99.4	91.8	7.6	59
Mar.	244.6	158.0	3.0	155.0	166.7	19.2	147.5	97.1	89.6	7.5	60
Apr.	244.8	155.8	2.9	152.9	164.9	19.4	145.5	99.3	91.9	7.4	59
May	241.9	150.7	3.8	146.9	158.6	20.8	137.8	104.1	95.0	9.1	57
June	239.7	147.1	2.7	144.4	155.9	19.2	136.7	103.0	95.3	·7.7	57

[1]Revised series. [2]Estimated weighted-average price of retail cuts from Choice Yield Grade 3 carcass. [3]Value of carcass-quantity equivalent to 1 lb of retail cuts. A wholesale-carcass equivalent of 1.464 was used prior to 1970; it was increased gradually to 1.476 in 1976 and later years. [4]Portion of gross carcass value attributed to fat and bone trim. [5]Gross carcass value minus carcass byproduct allowance. [6]Market value to producer for 2.4 lb of live animal, equivalent to 1 lb of retail cuts. [7]Portion of gross farm value attributed to edible and inedible byproducts. [8]Gross farm value minus farm byproduct allowance. [9]Percent net farm value is of retail price. [10]ERS data through May 1981, BLS series since June.

Table 43.—Pork: Retail, wholesale, and farm values, spreads, and farmers' share[1]

Year	Retail price[2]	Wholesale value[3]	Gross farm value[4]	Byproduct allowance[5]	Net farm value[6]	Farm-retail spread			Farmers' share[7]
						Total	Wholesale-retail	Farm-wholesale	
					Cents per lb				*Percent*
1979	144.1	100.4	72.2	5.6	66.6	77.5	43.7	33.8	46
1980	139.4	98.0	68.3	5.1	63.2	76.2	41.4	34.8	45
1981[8]	152.4	106.7	75.5	5.2	70.3	82.1	45.7	36.4	46
1982	175.4	121.8	94.3	6.3	88.0	87.4	53.6	33.8	50
1983	169.8	108.9	81.4	4.9	76.5	93.3	60.9	32.4	45
1983									
I	183.0	119.3	93.8	5.7	88.1	94.9	63.6	31.3	48
II	171.1	106.9	79.6	4.9	74.7	96.4	64.2	32.2	44
III	165.4	105.6	79.6	5.0	74.7	90.7	59.8	30.9	45
IV	159.8	103.8	72.8	4.3	68.5	91.3	56.0	35.3	43
1984									
I	161.5	108.6	81.3	5.6	75.7	85.8	52.9	32.9	47
II	159.4	109.5	83.3	6.1	77.2	82.2	49.9	32.3	49
1984									
Jan.	162.2	112.9	84.8	5.5	79.3	82.9	49.3	33.6	49
Feb.	162.9	109.2	79.0	5.4	73.6	89.3	53.7	35.6	45
Mar.	159.4	103.8	80.1	6.0	74.1	85.3	55.6	29.7	46
Apr.	159.8	107.1	82.1	6.1	76.0	83.8	52.7	31.1	48
May	158.6	110.6	81.7	6.1	75.6	83.0	48.0	35.0	48
June	159.9	110.8	86.1	6.1	80.0	79.9	49.1	30.8	50

[1]Revised series. [2]Estimated weighted-average price of retail cuts from pork carcass. [3]Value of wholesale quantity equivalent to 1 lb of retail cuts. A wholesale-carcass equivalent of 1.06 is used for all years. [4]Market values to producer for 1.7 lb. of live animal, equivalent to 1 lb of retail cuts. [5]Portion of gross farm value attributable to edible and inedible byproducts. [6]Gross farm value minus byproduct allowance. [7]Percent net farm value is of retail price. [8]ERS data through May 1981, BLS series since June.

Second-Half Consumption To Fall And Prices To Increase

Per capita red meat and poultry consumption during the second half is expected to be 3 to 5 percent below year-earlier levels. Beef consumption is projected to decline 3 to 5 percent, while pork may slip 8 to 10. Broiler consumption is expected to gain about 4 percent and turkey consumption to decline about 1 percent.

Total red meat and poultry consumption in first-quarter 1985 is expected to fall slightly from a year earlier. The largest drop will be in pork, with a year-over-year decline of about 7 percent. Beef consumption is expected to fall about 4 percent, while broiler consumption may rise 5 percent. Turkey consumption should be unchanged.

Table 44.—Young chicken supply and utilization, 1982-85[1]

Year	Total production[2]	Beginning stocks	Total supply	Ending stocks	Exports and shipments	Military	Civilian disappearance	
							Total	Per pita
				Million pounds				*Pounds[3]*
1982[2] Year	12,174.7	32.6	12,207.3	22.3	648.5	34.0	11,502.5	50.0
1983[4]								
I	3,062.3	22.3	3,084.6	20.9	147.0	7.8	2,908.9	12.6
II	3,275.8	20.9	3,296.7	20.8	141.8	8.8	3,125.3	13.5
III	3,138.5	20.8	3,159.3	26.0	132.0	9.2	2,992.0	12.9
IV	2,923.8	26.0	2,949.8	21.2	142.7	7.1	2,778.7	11.9
Year	12,400.4	22.3	12,422.7	21.2	563.6	33.0	11,804.9	50.8
1984[4]								
I	3,088.4	21.2	3,109.6	14.4	124.2	6.7	2,964.4	12.7
II	3,334.6	14.4	3,349.0	17.4		10.7		
Year[5]	12,767.0	21.2	12,788.0	20.0	534.0	38.0	12,196.0	52.0
1985 Year[5]	13,362.0	20.0	13,382.0	20.0	510.0	37.0	12,815.0	54.1

[1]Totals may not add because of rounding. [2]Total production is estimated by multiplying the Federally inspected slaughter by the ratio of the annual total production to the annual Federally inspected slaughter. The ratio for 1984-85 is the same as in 1983. [3]Calculated from unrounded data. [4]Preliminary. [5]Projected.

Table 45.—Mature chicken supply and utilization, 1982-85[1]

Year	Total production[2]	Beginning stocks	Total supply	Ending stocks	Exports and shipments	Domestic disappearance		
						Military	Civilian disappearance	
							Total	Per capita
				Million pounds				*Pounds[3]*
1982 Year	744.5	116.5	861.0	112.7	26.3	2.2	719.7	3.1
1983[4]								
I	207.0	112.7	319.7	115.2	5.3	2.0	197.2	.9
II	188.5	115.2	303.7	123.2	7.2	.4	172.8	.7
III	170.7	123.2	293.9	113.0	8.6	.5	171.8	.7
IV	149.2	113.0	262.2	91.6	6.7	.3	163.6	.7
Year	715.4	112.7	828.1	91.6	27.9	3.2	705.5	3.0
1984[4]								
I	161.1	91.6	252.7	92.4	5.8	.4	154.1	.7
II	189.9	92.4	282.4	104.8		.7		
Year[5]	690.0	91.6	781.0	110.0	23.0	1.0	646.0	2.8
1985 Year[5]	771.0	110.0	881.0	110.0	20.0	1.0	750.0	3.2

[1]Totals may not add because of rounding. [2]Total production is estimated by multiplying the Federally inspected slaughter by the ratio of the annual total production to the annual Federally inspected slaughter. The ratio for 1984-85 is the same as in 1983. [3]Calculated from unrounded data. [4]Preliminary. [5]Projected.

With the likelihood of smaller red meat supplies, increasing consumer incomes, and a strong economy, retail prices are expected to rise through the remainder of 1984 and first-half 1985. The largest gains in retail prices in the last half of 1984 are expected in pork. Declining year-over-year supplies in second-half 1984 will likely cause retail pork prices to rise about 8 to 12 percent from the first-half average of $1.60 a pound. Retail beef prices are expected to increase about 2 percent from the first half's $2.42 a pound. The increase in beef prices will probably be dampened in the second half, since beef production will remain near first-half levels until fall.

The largest gains in first-half 1985 are expected in pork. However, the moderate increase in broiler supplies may also hold down the retail price increases for beef and pork. Retail beef prices may rise 3 to 5 percent in 1985. Retail pork prices may increase 10 to 14 percent from this year's average.

Table 46.—Turkey supply and utilization, 1982-85[1]

Year	Total production[2]	Beginning stocks	Total supply	Ending stocks	Exports and shipments	Military	Civilian disappearance Total	Per capita[3]
			Million pounds					Pounds
1982 Year	2,505.5	238.4	2,743.9	203.9	55.6	12.1	2,472.3	10.7
1983[4]								
I	474.7	203.9	678.6	185.3	11.8	2.2	479.3	2.1
II	597.3	185.3	782.6	255.7	11.4	3.3	512.2	2.2
III	781.5	255.7	1,037.2	432.2	14.5	5.3	585.2	2.5
IV	780.2	432.2	1,212.4	161.8	16.2	2.6	1,031.8	4.4
Year	2,633.7	203.9	2,837.6	161.8	53.8	13.4	2,608.5	11.2
1984[4]								
I	444.1	161.8	605.9	149.4	5.8	1.7	449.0	1.9
II	601.6	149.4	750.9	226.6		3.9		
Year[5]	2,565.0	161.8	2,726.0	150.0	36.0	16.0	2,524.0	10.8
1985 Year[5]	2,702.0	150.0	2,852.0	175.0	42.0	17.0	2,618.0	11.1

[1]Totals may not add because of rounding. [2]Total production is estimated by multiplying the Federally inspected slaughter by the ratio of the annual total production to the annual Federally inspected slaughter. The ratio used in 1984-85 is the same as in 1983. [3]Calculated from unrounded data. [4]Preliminary. [5]Projected.

Table 47.—Total red meat supply and utilization by quarters, carcass and retail weight, 1982-85[1]

Year	Commercial production	Farm production	Beginning stocks	Imports	Total supply	Exports	Shipments	Military purchases	Ending stocks	Total disappearance	Per capita disappearance Carcass weight	Retail weight	Population
					Million lbs							Pounds	Millions
Beef:													
1982	25,366.00	170.00	257.00	1,939.18	24,732.18	249.74	55.30	135.00	294.00	23,988.13	104.28	77.17	231.10
1983[2]													
I	5,527.00	64.00	294.00	527.89	6,412.89	66.81	10.35	28.00	299.00	6,008.73	25.95	19.20	231.50
II	5,556.00	27.00	299.00	516.67	6,398.67	61.96	10.27	34.00	254.00	6,038.44	26.02	19.22	232.00
III	6,015.00	28.00	254.00	539.04	6,836.04	71.62	9.14	34.00	268.00	6,453.28	27.74	20.53	232.60
IV	5,962.00	64.00	268.00	347.47	6,641.47	71.71	10.47	25.00	325.00	6,209.29	26.66	19.73	233.20
Year	23,060.00	183.00	294.00	1,931.07	25,468.07	272.10	40.23	121.00	325.00	24,709.74	106.38	78.72	232.30
1984[3]													
I	5,708.00	61.00	325.00	470.46	6,564.46	90.04	10.81	24.00	326.00	6,113.61	26.16	19.36	233.70
II	5,819.00	26.00	326.00					36.00	304.00				234.20
Year[4]	22,978.00	175.00	325.00	1,775.00	25,253.00	290.00	56.00	115.00	275.00	24,517.00	104.60	77.40	234.50
1985[4]													
Year	22,375.00	175.00	275.00	1,800.00	24,625.00	320.00	60.00	100.00	300.00	23,845.00	100.70	74.50	236.80

Continued—footnotes at end of table

Year	Commercial production	Farm production	Beginning stocks	Imports	Total supply	Exports	Shipments	Military purchases	Ending stocks	Total disappearance	Carcass weight	Retail weight	Population
					Million lbs						Pounds		Millions
Pork:													
1982	14,121.00	108.00	264.00	612.11	15,105.11	214.29	151.16	96.00	219.00	14,424.66	62.68	59.03	231.10
1983[2]													
I	3,483.00	29.00	219.00	179.52	3,910.52	44.00	34.27	22.00	235.00	3,575.25	15.44	14.51	231.50
II	3,771.00	12.00	235.00	175.79	4,193.79	71.78	31.73	25.00	280.00	3,785.28	16.31	15.33	232.00
III	3,657.00	12.00	280.00	169.08	4,118.08	42.48	27.78	21.00	210.00	3,816.82	16.41	15.42	232.60
IV	4,206.00	29.00	210.00	177.22	4,622.22	61.06	47.82	21.00	301.00	4,191.34	17.99	16.91	233.20
Year	15,117.00	82.00	219.00	701.61	16,119.61	219.32	141.60	89.00	301.00	15,368.69	66.15	62.19	232.30
1984[3]													
I	3,737.00	29.00	301.00	201.87	4,268.87	49.03	38.88	20.00	351.00	3,809.96	16.30	15.33	233.70
II	3,670.00	12.00	351.00					28.00	406.00				234.20
Year[4]	14,432.00	82.00	301.00	875.00	15,690.00	190.00	140.00	88.00	300.00	14,972.00	63.80	60.00	234.50
1985[4]													
Year	14,100.00	82.00	300.00	850.00	15,332.00	200.00	140.00	80.00	275.00	14,637.00	61.80	58.10	236.80
Lamb and mutton:													
1982	356.00	9.00	11.00	18.67	394.67	1.72	2.42	1.00	9.00	380.52	1.65	1.66	231.10
1983[2]													
I	93.00	2.00	9.00	4.33	108.33	.27	.72	0.00	8.00	99.34	.43	.38	231.50
II	89.00	2.00	8.00	5.89	104.89	.49	.87	0.00	9.00	94.53	.40	.36	232.00
III	94.00	2.00	9.00	5.99	110.99	.24	.34	0.00	9.00	101.41	.43	.39	232.60
IV	91.00	2.00	9.00	2.56	104.56	.45	.29	0.00	11.00	92.82	.40	.35	233.20
Year	367.00	8.00	9.00	18.77	402.77	1.45	2.22	0.00	11.00	388.10	1.66	1.48	232.30
1984[3]													
I	98.00	3.00	11.00	3.19	115.19	.45	.47	0.00	8.00	106.27	.45	.33	233.70
II	92.00	2.00	8.00					0.00	9.00				234.20
Year[4]	355.00	10.00	11.00	20.00	396.00	3.00	2.00	1.00	9.00	381.00	1.60	1.40	234.50
1985[4]													
Year	320.00	10.00	9.00	20.00	359.00	3.00	2.00	1.00	9.00	344.00	1.50	1.30	236.80
Veal:													
1982	423.00	25.00	9.00	18.76	475.76	3.80	1.47	6.00	7.00	457.49	1.98	1.64	231.10
1983[2]													
I	103.00	9.00	7.00	8.54	127.54	.98	.18	2.00	7.00	117.38	.51	.42	231.50
II	98.00	3.00	7.00	5.19	113.19	1.13	.17	3.00	7.00	101.89	.44	.36	232.00
III	110.00	4.00	7.00	2.44	123.44	1.10	.42	1.00	9.00	111.92	.48	.40	232.60
IV	117.00	9.00	9.00	2.38	137.38	.85	.32	1.00	9.00	126.21	.54	.45	233.20
Year	428.00	25.00	7.00	18.55	478.55	4.06	1.09	7.00	9.00	457.40	1.97	1.64	232.30
1984[3]													
I	115.00	8.00	9.00	9.56	141.56	1.13	.53	0.00	10.00	129.90	.56	.41	233.70
II	113.00	4.00	10.00					1.00	8.00				234.20
Year[4]	434.00	24.00	9.00	25.00	492.00	4.00	1.00	5.00	7.00	476.00	2.00	1.70	234.50
1985[4]													
Year	385.00	24.00	7.00	25.00	441.00	4.00	0.00	7.00	7.00	423.00	1.80	1.50	236.80
Total red meat:													
1982	37,264.00	312.00	541.00	2,588.72	40,707.71	469.56	210.35	238.00	529.00	39,260.79	170.59	139.35	231.10
1983[2]													
I	9,206.00	104.00	529.00	720.28	10,559.28	112.06	45.52	52.00	549.00	9,800.70	42.32	34.52	231.50
II	9,514.00	44.00	549.00	703.54	10,810.54	135.36	43.04	62.00	550.00	10,029.14	43.18	35.32	232.00
III	9,876.00	46.00	550.00	716.55	11,188.55	115.44	37.68	56.00	496.00	10,483.43	45.07	36.74	232.60
IV	10,376.00	104.00	496.00	529.63	11,505.63	134.07	58.90	47.00	646.00	10,619.66	45.59	37.44	233.20
Year	38,972.00	298.00	529.00	2,670.00	42,469.00	496.93	185.14	217.00	646.00	40,923.93	176.16	144.02	232.30
1984[3]													
I	9,658.00	101.00	646.00	685.08	11,090.08	140.65	50.69	44.00	695.00	10,159.74	43.47	35.43	233.70
II	9,694.00	44.00	695.00					65.00	727.00				234.20
Year[4]	38,199.00	291.00	646.00	2,695.00	41,831.00	487.00	199.00	209.00	591.00	40,345.00	172.00	140.50	234.50
1985[4]													
Year	37,180.00	291.00	591.00	2,695.00	40,757.00	527.00	202.00	188.00	591.00	39,249.00	165.80	135.40	236.80

[1]Totals may not add because of rounding. [2]Revised. [3]Preliminary. [4]Forecast.

Table 48.—Total red meat and poultry supply and utilization, 1982-85[1]

Year	Total production	Beginning stocks	Imports	Total supply	Exports and shipments	Military	Ending stocks	Total civilian disappearance	Per capita disappearance
				Million pounds					Pounds
1982									
Year	53,003	929	2,589	56,520	1,410	286	868	53,956	203.3
1983[2]									
I	13,054	868	720	14,642	322	64	870	13,386	50.1
II	13,620	870	704	15,194	339	74	950	13,830	51.8
III	14,013	950	717	15,679	309	71	-1,066	14,233	52.9
IV	14,333	1,067	530	15,930	359	57	921	14,593	54.5
Year	55,019	868	2,670	58,557	1,328	267	921	56,042	209.2
1984[2]									
I	13,352	921	685	14,958	327	53	951	13,627	50.7
Year[3]	54,511	921	2,695	58,027	1,280	264	871	55,712	206.0
1985[3]									
Year	54,307	871	2,695	57,873	1,301	243	896	55,433	203.8

[1]Totals may not add due to rounding. [2]Preliminary. [3]Forecast.

Table 49.—Expenditures per person for red meat and poultry[1]

Year and quarter	Beef Expenditures	% of income	Pork Expenditures	% of income	Red meat Expenditures	% of income	Broilers Expenditures	% of income	Turkeys Expenditures	% of income	Poultry Expenditures	% of income	Total[2] Expenditures	% of income
					Dollars									
1979	176.36	2.42	91.18	1.25	267.54	3.67	32.26	0.44	8.82	0.12	41.09	0.56	308.62	4.23
1980	181.83	2.27	94.52	1.18	276.35	3.45	33.69	0.42	9.46	0.12	43.15	0.54	319.50	3.99
1981	184.16	2.10	98.68	1.13	282.84	3.23	35.93	0.41	10.24	0.12	46.00	0.53	329.01	3.75
1982	187.40	2.00	103.49	1.10	290.89	3.10	35.83	0.38	10.02	0.11	45.85	0.49	336.74	3.59
1983														
I	45.68	1.89	26.54	1.10	72.22	2.99	8.82	0.37	1.93	0.08	10.75	0.45	82.97	3.43
II	47.30	1.92	26.35	1.07	73.65	2.99	9.33	0.38	2.04	0.08	11.37	0.46	85.02	3.46
III	48.87	1.94	25.47	1.01	74.34	2.95	9.62	0.38	2.29	0.09	11.91	0.47	86.25	3.43
IV	45.53	1.77	27.01	1.05	72.54	2.82	9.21	0.36	4.00	0.16	13.21	0.52	85.75	3.33
Year	187.41	1.88	105.63	1.06	293.04	2.94	37.04	0.37	10.27	0.10	47.3I	0.47	340.35	3.41
1984														
I	47.06	1.77	24.71	0.93	71.77	2.70	10.77	0.41	1.79	0.07	12.56	0.48	84.33	3.18
II	46.97	1.74	24.07	0.89	71.04	2.63	11.19	0.41	2.03	0.08	13.22	0.49	84.26	3.12

[1]Red meat includes beef and pork only; poultry includes broilers and turkeys only. [2]Total includes beef, pork, broilers, and turkeys only.

Recent Shifts in the Location of U.S. Egg Production

Harold B. Jones, Jr.
and E. A. Ogden[1]

Abstract: Significant changes in the geographic location of egg production have occurred in the 1980's as production moves closer to grain and consumers. Some Southern States are losing share of production, while States in the Midwest and Mountain regions are gaining in output.

Keywords: Egg production, location, markets

The commercial egg industry is changing locations. Substantial production gains that occurred in the South Atlantic and South Central regions in the late 1950's and early 1960's continued throughout the 1970's. But, output in these regions apparently peaked in 1980. Egg production in the South has begun to drop. On the other hand, certain States in the Mid-Atlantic and East North Central regions are showing increases.

Those States with low volume production have always experienced marked percentage changes in output. Now, however, the size of new egg production complexes means that one or two producers can cause significant changes in any State.

In areas where output has dropped, much of the decline has been due to higher grain shipping costs. Producing areas where a large proportion of eggs are shipped long distances have also been vulnerable, since egg transportation costs have increased too.

Significant output increases have occurred in Indiana, Ohio, and Pennsylvania—States located in or near both the grain belt and many of the Nation's population centers. Some of the newer operations have been financed by foreign investors. Modern egg-producing operations are highly mechanized, with very large capital investments. Once investors begin to expand, there often is momentum toward additional investments in those areas.

Egg production has always been relatively decentralized, and markets are very competitive. Thus, higher transportation costs for grain and eggs in recent years have provided greater incentive for self-sufficiency in some areas that did not have a comparative advantage in egg production. The Mountain States are such an area. Thus, there is also a trend toward greater output in areas more remote from large population centers.

Both these shifts in production—to grain belt areas near population centers, and to remote regions increasing their self-sufficiency—may lead to lower costs for consumers if the production complexes are as efficient as those in established areas.

North Atlantic. This region's production remained relatively stable for many years up through 1980, with its share of U.S. egg production about 14 percent. (table A). Significant declines in egg production in 1980-83 occurred in all of the New England States except Connecticut. Production in New York and New Jersey also declined somewhat. However, Pennsylvania, the largest egg-producing State in the region, increased production 11 percent between 1980 and 1983, raising the share for the whole region. First-quarter changes for 1984 show that Connecticut, Rhode Island, and New Jersey increased production slightly, while in Pennsylvania avian flu has reduced output by nearly a fifth from the previous year.

Table A.—Regional trends in shares of production for eggs, U.S., selected years, 1950-1983

Region[1]	1950	1960	1970	1980	1981	1982	1983
	Percent						
North Atlantic	17.2	16.3	13.9	14.1	13.9	13.7	14.3
East North Central	19.9	17.6	13.7	14.0	14.8	15.7	16.1
West North Central	28.3	24.6	12.9	10.5	10.8	11.0	11.0
South Atlantic	8.8	13.2	20.9	24.8	21.7	21.6	21.1
South Central	14.9	14.3	21.4	21.7	21.2	20.5	19.9
Mountain	2.9	2.3	2.1	2.5	2.7	2.8	2.8
Pacific Coast	8.0	11.7	15.1	15.4	14.9	14.7	14.8
U.S. total	100.0	100.0	100.0	100.0	100.0	100.0	100.0
	Billion eggs						
U.S. production	58.9	61.5		68.1	69.5	69.6	69.5

[1]Regions based on U.S. Census Bureau definitions. *North Atlantic* includes Maine, N.H., Vt., Mass., Conn., R.I., N.Y., N.J., Pa.; *East North Central* includes Ohio, Ind., Ill., Mich., Wis.; *West North Central* includes Minn., Iowa, N. Dak., S. Dak., Nebr., Kans., Mo.; *South Atlantic* includes Del., Md., Va., W. Va., N.C., S.C., Ga., Fla.; *South Central* includes Ky., Tenn., Ala., Miss., Ark., La., Okla., Tex.; *Mountain* includes Mont., Idaho, Wyo., Colo., N. Mex., Ariz., Utah, Nev.; *Pacific Coast* includes Calif., Ore., Wash. Excludes Alaska and Hawaii.

East North Central. This region continued to increase egg production in the 1980's, a turnaround which began in the mid-1970's after many years of declining egg production. The region's share of U.S. production rose from 14.0 percent in 1980 to 16.1 percent in 1983. Production gained significantly in Indiana and Ohio, which are the region's major producing States. Illinois production continued to decline, whereas Michigan and Wisconsin were relatively stable, with only slight declines in 1983. For all the States except Michigan, first-quarter 1984

[1]Jones is an agricultural economist, Economic Research Service, stationed at the University of Georgia, Athens, where Ogden is a research assistant.

33

changes moved in the same direction as developments the preceding 3 years.

West North Central. Egg production in this region declined substantially for many decades. However, production has increased somewhat during 1980-83, and the region's share of U.S. output held at the 11.0 percent level in 1983. Production increased 12.8 percent in Minnesota, the major producing State in the region, between 1980 and 1983; there were significant gains in Kansas and North Dakota also. Iowa's production increased slightly, and South Dakota's and Nebraska's declined. In the first quarter of 1984, most States continued their earlier direction, although Iowa dropped and South Dakota increased slightly from the previous year.

South Atlantic. After many years of substantial increases, output apparently peaked in 1980 at 15.1 billion eggs or 21.8 percent of U.S. production. Regional production declined all 3 years from 1981 to 1983. Georgia, the leading producer in the region, dropped 17 percent between 1980 and 1983. Other States with output declines were South Carolina, Virginia, Florida, and West Virginia. Production increased in Delaware and Maryland. States have continued their individual trends in first-quarter 1984 except for Virginia and North Carolina, which gained slightly over the previous year, and Florida, which lost even more than in previous years.

South Central. This region's production also peaked in 1980, at 15.1 billion eggs or 21.7 percent of the U.S. total. Output dropped in each of the 3 years after 1980,

reaching 13.5 billion in 1983. Significant production declines have occurred in all of the major producing States except Texas and Oklahoma, where output is relatively stable. First-quarter 1984 figures show similar trends for individual States except for Alabama, which has increased production slightly, and Texas, which showed a significant drop from the previous year.

Mountain. This region's production declined for many years through the mid-1970's, but it has increased since then. Production climbed 8.5 percent from 1980 in 1983, to 1.9 billion eggs, only about 2.8 percent of U.S. output. Individual States' output is relatively small. However, Montana, Idaho, and Colorado have seen substantial increases. Significant declines have occurred in New Mexico, with Wyoming and Arizona showing somewhat smaller drops. First-quarter changes for 1984 show similar patterns except for Colorado and Utah, which showed losses from a year earlier.

Pacific Coast. After substantial increases in production in the 1950's and 1960's, this region's output was stable in the 1970's. Peak production was in 1980, at 10.7 billion eggs, or 15.4 percent of the U.S. total. Since 1980, output has slipped about 6.5 percent to 10.0 billion (14.8 percent of U.S. products) in 1983. California is the region's major producing State, and production there dropped 7.1 percent between 1980 and 1983. Production in Washington and Oregon has also declined slightly in the last few years. First-quarter 1984 shows increased production in California and Washington but a small decline in Oregon.

Figure 1

Egg Production by States for 1983 and Percentage Change in Production from 1980 to 1983

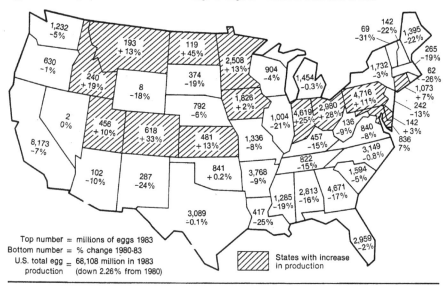

Top number = millions of eggs 1983
Bottom number = % change 1980-83
U.S. total egg = 68,108 million in 1983
production (down 2.26% from 1980)

States with increase in production

LIST OF TABLES

*U.S. GOVERNMENT PRINTING OFFICE : 1984 0-420-932/ERS-2229

H SUGAR AND SWEETNER
   ISSUED QUARTERLY ACCEPTED FOR ONE YEAR ONLY
   S/N 001-028-80016-8
H $8.00 PER SUBSCRIPTION FOR DOMESTIC MAILING
   $10.00 PER SUBSCRIPTION FOR FOREIGN MAILING

   SERVICES TERMINATE 03/84 COPIES 0001

2Q   H

       H

R 12/07/83

DO NOT WRITE ON THIS SIDE OTHER THAN IN SPACES INDICATED BELOW

[72 SAS 20250USDAESODUY   0001]

USDA EMS 41 31 DT 3 00500
KENT D MILLER
500 12TH ST S W
WASHINGTON   DC   20250

☐ REMMITTANCE ENCLOSED

☐ CHANGE QUANTITY TO _____

☐ CHANGE OF ADDRESS (OVER →)

IMPORTANT! RETURN THIS CARD IN ENCLOSED ENVELOPE TO RENEW SUBSCRIPTION

Credit Card No. | | | | | | | | | | | | | | | | | |

Expiration Date Month/Year | | | |

Deposit Account Number | | | | | | | ☐

SEEN ONE OF THESE LATELY ????

It's your renewal notice from the Government Printing Office.
You can expect it about 90 days before your subscription
expires. Since it's the ONLY notice you'll get, you need to
return it with your payment to ensure uninterrupted service.

If you misplaced the renewal notice, use the order form below.

(Cut along line)

••

*Mail this form to: Superintendent of Documents, Government Printing Office, Washington, D.C.. 20250

$_____ Amount

_____ Here is my check payable to the SUPERINTENDENT OF DOCUMENTS.

_____ Charge my GPO Deposit Account _____

_____ Charge my VISA or MASTERCARD Account _____

                               Expiration date _____

Charge orders may be telephoned to the GPO order desk at
(202) 783-3238 from 8 a.m. to 4 p.m. ET, Mon.-Fri. (except holidays).

RENEWAL **Livestock & Poultry Outlook & Situation Report**
            USDA Economic Research Service
            $15.00 U.S. $18.75 Foreign

Company or Person Name
| | | | | | | | | | | | | | | | | | | | | | | | | | | | | | | | |

Additional address/attention line
| | | | | | | | | | | | | | | | | | | | | | | | | | | | | | | | |

Street address
| | | | | | | | | | | | | | | | | | | | | | | | | | | | | | | | |

City   State   ZIP Code
| | | | | | | | | | | | | | | | | | | | | | | | | | | | | | | | |

(or Country)
| | | | | | | | | | | | | | | | | | | | | | | | | | | | | | | | |

PLEASE PRINT, TYPE, OR USE MAILING LABEL FROM BACK COVER

AGRICULTURAL OUTLOOK

Tracking the Business of Agriculture

Agricultural Outlook pools USDA's latest analyses of the agricultural economy in one comprehensive monthly package. Besides its regular outlook coverage—including commodity supply and demand, world agriculture and trade, food and marketing, farm inputs, agricultural policy, transportation and storage, and related developments in the general economy—Agricultural Outlook is USDA's official outlet for farm income and food price forecasts. While emphasizing short-term outlook information, the magazine also publishes special reports containing long-term analyses of topics ranging from international trade policies to U.S. land use and availability. Agricultural Outlook averages 48 pages and includes 6 pages of updated charts and 20 pages of statistical tables.

Order Now!

Agricultural Outlook Subscription Order Form

Enclosed is $ _____ ☐ check,
☐ money order, or charge to my
Deposit Account No.

☐☐☐☐☐☐☐–☐

Order No. _____

Mail to:
Superintendent of Documents
U.S. Government Printing Office
Washington, D.C. 20402

For Office Use Only	
Quantity	Charges
_____ Enclosed _____	
_____ To be mailed _____	
_____ Subscriptions _____	
Postage _____	
Foreign handling _____	
MMOB _____	
OPNR _____	
_____ UPNS	
_____ Discount	
_____ Refund	

Credit Card Orders Only

Total charges $_____ Fill in the boxes below.

Credit
Card No. ☐☐☐☐☐☐☐☐☐☐☐☐☐☐☐☐☐☐☐☐

Expiration Date
Month/Year ☐☐☐☐

Please enter my subscription to **Agricultural Outlook** (ARGO) for one year at $29.00 Domestic $36.25 Foreign.

| Name—First, Last |
| Company name or additional address line |
| Street address |
| City | State | ZIP Code |
| (or Country) |

PLEASE PRINT OR TYPE
Make checks payable to: Superintendent of Documents.

Japan To Increase Imports of U.S. Grains and Meats

"I am impressed with the quality and thoroughness of this work. It represents a real contribution to our understanding of Japanese agriculture."
Fred Sanderson, Guest Scholar, Brookings Institution.

Japan has long been one of the most important markets for U.S. agricultural exports, especially grains and oilseeds. A new report by USDA's Economic Research Service, *Japan's Feed-Livestock Economy: Prospects for the 1980's,* helps explain why that has been so and why future farm exports to Japan will probably rise even higher.

Each year, Japan purchases about 20 percent of total U.S. corn exports, 50 percent of U.S. sorghum exports, and more than 20 percent of U.S. soybean exports. By 1990, the United States may be able to increase its grain and soybean exports by a third and quintuple its beef exports, according to William Coyle, author of the report. In contrast, the Japanese market for imported dairy products, pork, and poultry will show little or no growth. The United States provides more than 65 percent of Japan's imports of coarse grains (corn, barley, sorghum), 95 percent of its soybean imports, and 71 percent of its soybean meal imports.

The report includes extensive tables and charts on Japanese consumption, production, and trade of beef, dairy, poultry, fish, and feed grains, including projections through 1990.

Japan's Feed-Livestock Economy: Prospects for the 1980's (William T. Coyle; $5.00; 80 pages, stock no. 001-000-04316-1) can be purchased from Superintendent of Documents, U.S. Government Printing Office, Washington, D.C. 20402. GPO pays the postage. Make check or money order payable to Superintendent of Documents.

For faster service, call GPO's order desk, (202) 783-3238, and charge your purchase to your VISA, MasterCard, or GPO Deposit account. Bulk discounts are available.

CPSIA information can be obtained
at www.ICGtesting.com
Printed in the USA
BVHW060849140119
537775BV00008B/1149/P